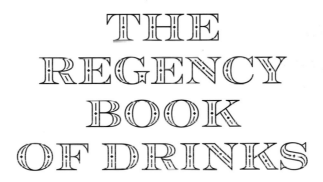

# THE
# REGENCY
# BOOK
# OF DRINKS

*I dedicate this book and any triumphs or mischief that it may inspire to a certain terrifying dowager—my dear friend, confidante, and loyal protector.*

*— Lady Thornwood*

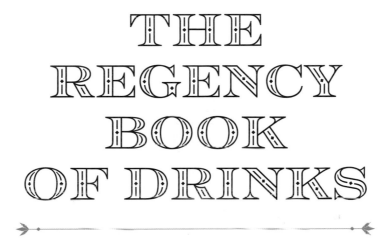

# THE REGENCY BOOK OF DRINKS

## QUAFFS, QUIPS, TIPPLES & TALES FROM GROSVENOR SQUARE

**Lady Thornwood**

ABRAMS IMAGE, NEW YORK

# CONTENTS

# PROLOGUE

**L**ONDON, THE SECOND DECADE OF THE NINETEENTH CENTURY.

Britannia shines illustrious, the wonder of the world. Rich. Powerful. And as the social season commences, decidedly decadent. It is the period we'll come to call "Regency," a polite nod toward unfortunate circumstances, those being of our beloved ruler, King George III, who finds himself grievously unwell, and his heir, the prince regent, who wields state power in his stead whilst George wanders the royal gardens blissfully none the wiser.

But in London's glittering ballrooms, where fates and fortunes are made—or broken—the king's wife, Queen Charlotte, reigns supreme.

How to conquer this tempestuous territory, this citadel of custom and manners, this battlefield of wit and wealth? Dear reader, consider the cocktail.

Wielded properly, a spirited libation can be a tool of social triumph—or devastation. Consummately elegant, it yet possesses wicked potential. And so one must choose wisely.

Let me, Lady Thornwood, be your guide, for I have quietly made myself a student of the cocktail's potent power. Gathered in these pages you'll find quaffs to besot the most hardened rake, tipples to soothe the most frazzled mama, and concoctions capable of extraordinary transfixion. Herein I shall instruct you in their proper use—the right remedy matched to scene and setting, be they public and pure or more private and . . . lively. I judge not.

With each drink, too, I offer its tantalizing tale—some are scandalous, some fortifying, all gleaned as I observed, ever watchful, the spirit world at work upon the denizens of the *ton*\*.

A certain duke's weakness? The sip that predisposed a debutante's debauching? All here, plus a dash of riveting tattle, apropos of the lives, loves, fancies, and foibles of some of London society's most intriguing—and notorious—characters. Enjoy.

As the Regency unfolds, ships sail up the Thames from every corner of the globe freighting tantalizing spices, vibrant fruits, and marvelous elixirs. Let us come to know this plenitude and craft it to our purpose. Cocktails stiffen the spine, unlock the tongue, and add sheen to the dullest drawing room.

*Coupes up!*

---

\*Not in the know? "*Ton*" is short for "*le bon ton*," reader, as in the *crème de la crème* of society. It is insider speak—and French, but one overlooks that small detraction.

## Chapter 1

# SETTING UP THE REGENCY BAR

An ambitious mama launching a young debutante or eligible bachelor upon the marriage mart is not dissimilar to a crafter of cocktails. The doyenne ruthlessly assesses her offspring's most alluring qualities—be they beguiling eyes, chestnut locks, a fine figure, or an ample fortune—then plays these to their utmost advantage. The cocktail maker does the same with spirits. Mama's tools are fashion, fabric, and word of a fat dowry. The cocktail maker has an array of mixing implements and fine glassware at their disposal.

But when all is said and done, <u>both</u> must trust in chemistry.

# A Panoply of Potables

Setting up the Regency bar begins with assembling an array of spirits. Even in these times of war and blockade, Britain's cocktail ingredients hail from every corner of the globe. Some require an intrepid spirit to procure: The element of danger only heightens their allure. Others are more quotidian, but no less intriguing.

With a well-stocked bar, one may mix a drink at a moment's notice, accentuating a spirit's finest features with a cascade of sweet, sharp, and even bitter flavours. When I am introduced to a fellow enthusiast's bar and behold a gleaming array of bottles and decanters—a veritable apothecary of intoxication!—I recognize a sophisticate and a kindred soul.

*Behold, dear reader, the spirit world . . .*

## HAIL, BRITANNIA

Despite its opulent seasonal attractions, city life is somewhat suspect amongst the *ton*. The truly well bred say they prefer the countryside, even if they're more apt to gawk in reverence at its pastoral stillness than to appreciate its ripe, rippling industry. Barley, glory of the British Isles, is the grain of our peerless native spirits: gin, Scotch, and Irish whiskey.

## · GIN ·

How far we've come since the dark days when mothers abandoned their children for drink and gin was the scourge of backstreet London. Today, properly made gin is regaining its respectability and possesses the same pleasing aromatic qualities that once made it the toast of the court of William and Mary.

### GIN TASTES OF . . .

Abundance. And botanicals, foremost amongst them juniper—from whence gin derives its name—along with a host of exotic peels, plants, roots, and bark. Gin is as bracing as a walk in the forest, woodsy notes balancing the perfume of lemon and orange peel, coriander seeds, cinnamon, and rose.

Our fighting men discovered genever battling Spain during the Eighty Years' War, called it "Dutch courage," and brought back a taste for it. It is distilled from malted barley wine, like Scotch, but steeped with botanicals, including juniper. To make an English "gin" we kept the botanicals but jettisoned the malt. Genever is bready, nutty, and earthy, with warm spices like clove, ginger, and nutmeg.

### STYLES OF GIN

#### Plymouth gin

Our era's most typical style is dry and somewhat earthy, with slightly less juniper and more citrus in the botanicals.

#### Old Tom

Akin to Dutch genever, Old Tom is sweeter and richer than Plymouth gin, with less heady botanical flavours. It harkens to London's notorious Puss & Mew gin shops, the ones with the black cat carvings—pop in a coin and out flowed gin from the cat's mouth!

#### Navy Strength

This gin is so strong, it is said gunpowder will still light even when wetted with it. Aboard ship, it is reserved for our gallant naval officers. In cocktails, it holds its own even when diluted.

## • SCOTCH •

The greater part of Scotland's whisky has been bootlegged to avoid the tax for almost a hundred years. Connoisseurship requires acquaintance with a dependable smuggler—thus, perhaps, the rake's natural affinity? The finest Scotch (illegally) procurable is well aged and made purely from malted barley. If not, it is best avoided, lest one tarnish one's reputation for disreputable discernment.

### SCOTCH TASTES OF . . .

Infamy. In truth, there is no singular "flavours" of Scotch. But its backbone is malted barley, which gives the spirit its fire, richness, and warmth. Characteristics, if not truly flavours.

*'Freedom and whisky gang thegither,*
*Tak aff your dram!'*

*—Robbie Burns, 1786*

Let us pause to remember the dearly departed Mr. Burns—a rake of the highest order.

A heavy crystal vessel is the way to store one's Scotch. Unlike port or sherry (which should be kept in darkened glass), distilled spirits won't be marred by light and air. They age only whilst in contact with wood in a barrel. Suitably, one hears that a certain viscount is never without his late father's crystal decanter when "working" in the study. (Though that faithful gentleman was, of course, a brandy drinker.)

## STYLES OF SCOTCH

### Maritime
Briny, smoky Scotches come from the rugged coast and islands. To varying degrees, the spirits taste of the peat fires used for drying malted barley.

### Highlands
They make bold, spicy Scotch with notes of honey and sometimes a gentle hint of smoke in the cold and windy highlands.

### Lowlands
Milder climes make for milder Scotch. The Speyside spirit tastes of honey, apples, vanilla, and spice. In the Lowlands (perhaps one has visited Gretna Green?) a dram tastes of grass, honeysuckle, and cream.

## · IRISH WHISKEY ·

Dublin's distillers have proven themselves the equal of any cunning mama. They've been sidestepping stills taxes for nearly a hundred years, and when the government recently attempted a new tax on malt, they simply rewrote their whiskey recipes! Now, in contrast to Scotch, Irish whiskey is distinctive for its use of "green" unmalted barley, and Dublin has become the capital of the kingdom's spirits industry.

### IRISH WHISKEY TASTES OF . . .

Ingenuity. Connoisseurs are calling Irish "single pot still" whiskey the best in the world, and, reader, I cannot say they are wrong. It is creamy, refined, mellow, and delightfully fruity.

> Pot stills are notoriously inefficient but make spirit with lots of character that ages beautifully. At the moment, they are also what we have got. But should Mr. Coffey, a Dublin distiller and tinkerer, get his continuous "column still" working, we may one day say his invention changed spirit-making forever.

## THE CONTINENT

Do we fight the French so incessantly because we cannot make our own wine?! Reader, it is not implausible. It seems no matter how many Shakespeares or Byrons England produces, we cannot vault beyond wine's cultural cachet. Thusly do the *ton's* young gentlemen go abroad for the Grand Tour—and bring home a taste for the Continent's brandies and wine-based spirits. All of which are, frankly, indispensable in cocktails.

> A good cellar is key to a good bar, as without Champagne there are no sparkling cocktails, whilst red, white, and rosé wines are all useful in various punches and low-potency drinks.

## • BRANDY •

All spirits distilled from fruit are brandies. But only a fool would offer "brandy" and serve less than a well-aged Cognac*, made from the finest Bordeaux wine.

## BRANDY TASTES OF . . .

Luxury. And fruit. Barrel aging Cognac for a minimum of two years creates a light, golden-toned, floral spirit. Between four and six years, it darkens and picks up vanilla and spice flavours, then shades amber and tastes of toffee. Older than that, Cognac turns mahogany in colour, with flavours like coconut, leather, and even cigars.

After he was felled by Napoleon's sniper at Trafalgar in 1805, Admiral Nelson's body was shipped back to England preserved in brandy. Even our greatest hero—even in death!—had a taste for French spirits.

The fabled vintages harkening to the Great Comet of 1811 are eagerly awaited. Still young, no doubt they'll soon begin to appear. Perhaps in time for the marriages of certain young gentlemen with a fondness for Continental travel?

*Whither, then, the English name for a spirit that is so consummately French? It was first made in France by Dutch traders, who called it *brandwijn*, or "burnt wine." Aboard British trading ships, *brandwijn* became simply "brandy." Point, England.

## • THE FORTIFIED WINES •

Sherry, port, and Madeira are so familiar, they're practically English at this point. And given their low potency, even an innocent may sip one without scandal. They are made by introducing brandy, which "fortifies" and keeps the wine from spoiling during long ocean transport.

One hears the signing of the Declaration of Independence was celebrated with a Madeira toast, a surprisingly elegant gesture given the Americans' fondness for histrionics.

## STYLES OF FORTIFIED WINES

### Sherry
One finds this tipple on the coast of southern Spain. Manzanilla and fino sherries are dry, nutty, and floral in flavour. Olorosso and PX sherries are rich and complex.

### Port
Hailing from Portugal, port is made with a base wine so undrinkable, were it not for England's desperation to import any wine a few centuries back, port may never have developed at all. Tawny port has nutty, apricot flavours. Ruby ports are rich, sweet, and fruity.

### Madeira
Named after its birthplace—a Portuguese island sitting on the East Indies trade route—this spirit ranges from sweet to dry. But for cocktails, try bottles labeled "rainwater," which is medium dry, fruity, and citrusy.

## • VERMOUTH •

Bonaparte's ambition ravages the Continent's borders, but in Savoy*, the vermouth making continues. A fortified wine infused with roots and botanicals, vermouth is absolutely essential to any well-provisioned bar.

"Vermouth" comes from the German *wermut,* meaning "wormwood," which all vermouth contains. In service of science, however, let me dispel the rumour that wormwood causes delirium. Reader, it is alcohol—in excessive amounts—that causes delirium. Enjoy your vermouth**.

## STYLES OF VERMOUTH

### Sweet
Hailing from Turin on the kingdom's Italian side, sweet vermouth is the court quaff of the Duke of Savoy. It can be bitter and tastes of spice, jammy fruits, and citrus zest.

### Dry
This French-style vermouth is crisp and acidic. Depending on the maker—Mr. Noilly and Mr. Dolin are two notables—it may be quite dry or very slightly sweet.

### Blanc
Pioneered by Mr. Dolin, this delightful quaff is less spicy than Turin-style sweet vermouth and less acidic than French dry. It is lush, rich, and full bodied.

*It bridges France and Italy, reader.

**In point of fact, the same goes for absinthe, but the Swiss liqueur is much more potent in much smaller doses than vermouth. In the right circles, one should simply pretend not to know that absinthe is merely intoxicating, not mind-altering, and enjoy the opportunity for inhibition.

## • LIQUEURS •

I acquire liqueurs on my travels the way other ladies of the *ton* amass perfume or silk stockings. These are sweetened spirits infused with secret blends of roots and botanicals.

Some favourites appear in this book, including a gentian-laced bitter aperitif I found in the French Auvergne, and Ramazzotti, a brand-new *digestivo* from Italy. There is a cherry liqueur from Denmark; Swiss absinthe that tastes of anise; curaçao (named for the bitter orange) from the Bols distillery in Amsterdam; a sweet and nutty tipple made from cherry pits in the Istrian part of Italy; various fruit liqueurs (very common in France); and Drambuie, a Scottish honey liqueur once brewed for Bonnie Prince Charlie. Finally, representing the French monastic tradition (every other edifice seems to produce its own signature liqueur!), I include two herbaceous elixirs, Benedictine and Chartreuse.

All liqueurs add nuance and sweetness to cocktails. The joy of the cocktail student is to experiment at will, for even small additions or substitutions can transform a drink entirely. Onward!

## THE AMERICAN EXPERIMENT

Following our latest skirmish* with the Americans, there are those in the *ton* who would have us shun the States entirely. This seems not only improbable but unreasonable, if for no other reason than the former colonies produce some delightful barrel-aged whiskies made with sweet corn and rye.

*The Americans are celebrating it with a new tune about their star-spangled flag. See my earlier note about Madeira.

## • BOURBON •

I consider this sweet Kentucky whiskey America's native spirit, for no other whiskey in the world uses corn so well. Bourbon becomes softer and more delicate when made with a high quantity of wheat; when there is a good amount of rye, it adds spicy dryness. I quite like the "wheated" style.

The county at the heart of Kentucky's whiskey production is called Bourbon, thus the spirit's name. Alas, a French connection.

## • RYE WHISKEY •

I adore this brown spirit for its bold, spicy style. Rye can be quite potent, and as the potency increases, so, too, does the spiciness. Some makers use nearly as much corn as rye in the recipe, which makes it nearly as sweet as Bourbon. I prefer the "high rye" formulations.

When enthusiasts speak of "Monongahela whiskey," they are simply speaking of rye, reader. The whiskey gets this moniker from the river that threads through the northeastern states, where at this moment it is primarily made.

## THE WEST INDIES

For three centuries, every European power—and an accompanying restless horde of privateers, scoundrels, mercenaries, and adventurers—has been drawn to the green islands and azure seas of the Caribbean. For what? Sugar. And rum, the world's most notorious spirit.

If the ancient world order was built on salt, we have built ours upon sugar, reader. The struggle to liberate, elevate, and make reparations to our African brethren is urgent and <u>must</u> continue. To this day slavery persists in our colonies and in America. It is nothing less than a stain upon history.

## · RUM ·

Like Scotch, rum has no single flavour: Depending on how and where it is made, it can be grassy, floral, earthy, sweet, or even spiced. But one can say that where you find Englishmen in the Caribbean—in particular on Jamaica and Barbados—you find darker, fruitier, heavy-bodied rums that often taste strongly of molasses. In general, those are the rums I call for in this book.

If there is such a thing as an actually "English" rum, it is one called Pusser's, blended of five Guyanese rums, the same formulation doled out in daily tots to the Royal Navy. I call for it herein, too.

## · SIMPLE SYRUP ·

Many cocktails based on sugar-plantation punches require citrus to sharpen the drink and balance its sweetness. This puts one's orangerie to good use. Oranges, limes, lemons, and grapefruits are all called for in this book's recipes. For sweetness, in place of sugar lumps, one should make a batch of "simple" syrup.

### HERE IS HOW ONE DOES IT:

Mix equal parts of sugar and boiling water together until the crystals are dissolved. For example, 1 cup (200 g) sugar for 1 cup (240 ml) boiling water. When the syrup is prepared, one may store it in a jar or crockery and keep it cool. It will last for several weeks.

# The Libertine's Laboratory

I adore science, a subject foolishly deemed solely a man's purview[*]. For years, I have quietly followed the investigations of the academy with as much interest as I do the comings and goings of the *ton*. Therein was born my love of drinks. For cocktails are, truth be told, products of science.

## TOOLS AND TECHNIQUES

There are three basic styles of cocktails. There are those assembled (we say "built") in their serving glass: They require no further equipment than the jigger and perhaps a teaspoon to give the drink 5 to 6 stirs.

Then there are stirred drinks, for which a crystal or glass mixing vessel and a long metal barspoon are the requisite tools. These look appealingly like ornate laboratory equipment and give one's endeavours an academic flair, but their form is not incidental. The material is purposeful.

A superlative cocktail begins with careful measurement. For this, one needs a jigger: a small tool marked in increments of a quarter ounce. The best are two sided: a smaller cup on the top, a larger cup on the bottom. The smallest increment measured should be ¼ ounce (7.5 ml), the largest 1½ or 2 ounces (45 or 60 ml).

Beyond careful measurement, though, successful cocktail making depends on bringing drinks to their proper temperature—the degree at which the aromas and flavours of the particular cocktail are freed to play. Most drinks are served chilled, but the state of chilliness is a spectrum, not an end point. Enter the most important tool of cocktail making, which is ice, a catalyst not unlike the chemist's flame, and happily available throughout the year thanks to the miracle of our icehouses.

---

[*]See the abysmal understanding of human procreation held by most unwed women, a deficiency which ultimately harms gentlemen quite as much as it harms womankind!

To separate ice from liquid, one usually pours a stirred cocktail into its glass through a tool commonly called a "julep strainer," which looks like a handled shallow bowl pierced with small holes.

Solid 1-inch (2.5-cm) cubes of ice frozen in a mold are also very useful, as these work well for making drinks and stack cleanly into most glassware when it's time to serve.

### • AN EXPERIMENT •

To understand why one wants a crystal or glass vessel rather than a container of metal (such as tin or copper), try stirring a cocktail in each—glass and metal. You will discover that even when filled with ice and spirits, in comparison to the metal container the crystal or glass vessel is slow to chill. Thusly, whilst slowing stirring for about 25 to 30 stirs, much of the ice remains unmelted. The mixture becomes quite chilled but only lightly diluted. For a stirred cocktail, this is the ideal.

In cocktails, the most useful size for a piece of ice is somewhat big—either a hefty shard cracked from a solid block of ice using a pick or a solid cube of about 1½ to 2 inches (4 to 5 cm) square: Enthusiasts call these "rocks."

When a smaller size of ice is required—as for drinks served with copious amounts of cracked or crushed ice—rocks can be smashed and shattered: Wrap them in a cloth, then hammer with a metal or wooden mallet.

When serving a drink "on" the rocks—meaning over a piece of large ice—if the rock is too large to fit easily in the bottom of a cocktail's glass, either use a pick to break up the shard or use a knife's edge to taper the cube's form until it nestles cleanly.

The third technique is quite new to the craft of cocktails, but currently circulating amongst devoted practitioners like myself. It allows a cocktail mixture to become even more chilled than a stirred drink, with a degree more of dilution, and delightful tiny bubbles. We call the technique "shaking" and it requires a "shaker."

In Paris, intrepid aficionados are crafting metal shakers consisting of a large cup topped with a pierced lid and cap. From the city of Boston in America, one hears of a shaker that consists of a metal cup interlocked with a second vessel of glass.

### • AN EXPERIMENT •

As revealed in our stirring experiment, when filled with a large quantity of ice and cocktail ingredients, the metal shaker grows cold quickly. In consequence—there must be a thermodynamic principle at play?—as the container is violently agitated back and forth for about 15 to 20 seconds, a portion of the ice melts somewhat rapidly, adding slightly more dilution than one gets in a stirred drink. When a shaken drink is poured out, an icy cold and ever-so-lightly frothy drink is revealed.

*Huzzah!*

Ice chips are the ruination of a shaken drink, and neither the pierced cap of a Paris-style shaker nor what is commonly called a "Hawthorne strainer" is truly up to the task of filtering these from one's cocktail. Thusly one should pour a shaken drink through the Paris cap or the Hawthorne strainer into a fine-mesh tea strainer suspended above one's glass. Double straining ensures one's cocktail is of the requisite clarity, and that no ice or other imperfection slips into the drink, undoing all one's hard work.

# Adorn with Restraint

Audacity and tastelessness are often confused for twins.
There is a word for the debutante who enters the ballroom
draped in jewels and feathers and ribbons and blooms, reader:
"tawdry." Let not the same be said of your cocktail. Most
cocktails benefit from a final flourish, but I urge you, use
a delicate hand. I recommend the following.

### · FRESH HERBS FROM THE GARDEN ·

A single perfect mint leaf, for example, adds a refreshing aroma when the drink
is sipped. When a more substantial amount of mint is called for, pinch the end-
tip from a fresh sprig.

### · GRATED SPICE ·

Nutmeg and cinnamon smell like freshly made biscuits. Scrape the whole spices
against a hand-held grater to deposit a light flurry across the surface of the
cocktail. Typically, this is reserved for cocktails with a frothy or creamy top.

### · CITRUS PEEL ·

The outermost layer of peel is suffused with aromatic oils. For cocktail garnishes, cut a very thin swatch of peel about ¾ of an inch (2 cm) wide and
anywhere from 2 to 4 inches (5 to 10 cm) long, taking care not to dig into the
bitter white pith. Before adding to the drink, gently squeeze the peel in half,
lengthwise, over the cocktail's surface, "expressing" the oils so they spray across
the drink's surface, then rub the peel around the rim of the glass. Stirred and
built cocktails in particular benefit from this treatment.

## • FRUIT AND CITRUS •

A fresh fruit garnish is most appropriate when the recipe includes muddled fruit or when one has used fruited liqueurs in one's cocktail—a fresh raspberry in a drink with raspberry liqueur, for example. Other recipes benefit from a citrus wedge or wheel when citrus appears in the drink.

---

### • THE CONSUL'S CANDIED CHERRIES •

*Traveling abroad, I met an Italian consul who makes liqueur from sour Marasca cherry pits. As one who shares my love of drinks, he offered me his favourite fruit garnish: pitted cherries candied in a delectable syrup. I've found them easy enough to prepare myself at home (and yes, I do mean myself). They go beautifully in drinks made with brown spirits.*

---

Mix the sugar and water together in a medium-sized pot and stir to dissolve. Heat the mixture to boiling, then add the pitted cherries, reduce the heat, and simmer for 2 to 3 minutes at most (overcook the fruit and you've instead made jam). Stir in the brandy, then transfer the cherries and syrup to a lidded jar or crockery. Set aside in cold storage until ready to use.

**1½ cups (295 g) granulated sugar**

**6 ounces (180 ml) water**

**1 pound (455 g) pitted cherries (sour preferred, sweet acceptable)**

**8 ounces (240 ml) brandy**

---

### • EDIBLE FLOWERS •

A single, perfect rose petal poised upon the surface of a cocktail is simple and stunning. A smattering of geranium petals is also lovely, as are dainty violets or a small pansy, a pert clover blossom, tiny daisies, or showy fuschia from the hothouse. Be sensible, reader: If a flower is toxic when eaten, it belongs not in one's drink.

And again, restraint! If one's drink in any way resembles the fabrics favoured by a certain Grosvenor Square family, or attracts bees, one has gone too far.

Remember, a rose petal's hue speaks volumes. Shades of blush and pink are for the first days of a new romance. Red means passion. Burgundy, simplicity and refinement. White, perfection. And yellow? Jealousy and infidelity. Deploy with care!

# The Language of Glassware

Finally, reader, never forget—each cocktail tells a story, complete with aim and objective. Some drinks are bold and daring. Others demure. There are friendly cocktails, familial cocktails, and ones meant to seduce. The wrong glass—too clumsy, common, cavern-ous, or cute—will undo all of one's assiduous endeavours, like a wooden clog where a satin slipper is warranted.

When setting up the bar, one should equip oneself with a diverse selection of the following glass styles.

## • The Coupe •

**5 to 7 ounces (150 to 210 ml)**
a small bowl-shaped glass, said to have perfectly
fitted one of Marie Antoinette's breasts

# • The Flute •

**6 to 7 ounces (180 to 210 ml)**
most commonly associated with Champagne,
excellent for sparkling cocktails

# • The Goblet •

**8 to 10 ounces (240 to 300 ml)**
rather like a white wine glass, but with more heft,
good for drinks served on the rocks

## • The Balloon •

**18 to 24 ounces (540 to 720 ml)**
as one uses for drinking red wines,
rather oversized for holding iced drinks

## • The Rocks Glass •

**10 to 13 ounces (300 to 390 ml)**
a somewhat squat tumbler, sized to hold
a single large rock of ice

## • The Highball Glass •

**12 to 14 ounces (360 to 420 ml)**
tall, slender, and cylindrical, commonly used
for fizzy cocktails

## • The Punch Cup •

**8 to 10 ounces (240 to 300 ml)**
one will want a set to match one's punchbowl

Regarding glassware decoration: filigree, intricate stems, delicate etching, cut crystal—they all have their place. Match the glass to your mood or intention when choosing amongst flourishes. For example, I contemplate the person with whom I shall be drinking, and ask myself, "Lover or friend? Companion or conquest? Conspirator or nemesis?" then select the glass accordingly. This compass has always seen me true.

As has this final word of advice, applicable to cocktails, the London season, and marriage, equally: One who prepares in haste has ample time for regret.

*Good luck!*

## Chapter 2

# THE EVENING SOIRÉE

## SPARKLING SIPS FOR GLITTERING GATHERINGS

To the poets, birdsong and laughter have the ring of happiness. But to my ears, no sound is more mirthful than the crush of gravel under carriage wheels, for it means a party is afoot. Debutantes pour forth, cheeks flushed, and soon the dance floor is a swirl of silks and satin. Whilst around the edges, bejeweled mamas stalk their favoured prey, the advantageous match.

A good party is like a cake, sweet and satisfying. A great party is like a towering soufflé teetering just on the brink of collapse, all the more entertaining for the threat of imminent disaster. In the world of drinks, reader, nothing promulgates this mood quite like a sparkling cocktail.

Deceptively potent, the quintessential sparkling cocktail gains strength from two intoxicating ingredients, each a pleasure in its own right, together a tour de force—Champagne and spirit. Certain concoctions even slip a small spoonful of liqueur into the mix. The effect is bewitching. But proceed with temperance, innocents: When these cocktails are consumed without caution, the aura of giddy heedlessness quickly deteriorates into abject dismay—a state which may or may not be your aim.

Deploy the sparkling cocktail like Wellington marshaling his forces at Waterloo: strategically. As wraps slip from milky shoulders in the front hall, have a glass at the ready. Pass another as the evening builds toward crescendo. And should first light find your party still ablaze—a very good evening indeed—a bold and bubbly quaff is just the thing to toast the new day.

# Your Grace

Old and young, married or not, many a woman of uncontested virtue has fallen—repeatedly!—all on account of a certain dashing duke, known to be <u>at least</u> as passionate as this exquisite sparkler. Reader, well-bred women are seldom allowed to leer, but the private realms of our minds cannot be scrutinized.

1½ ounces (45 ml) **Old Tom gin**

¾ ounce (22.5 ml) **Fresh Pineapple Syrup (see page 159)**

½ ounce (15 ml) **lemon juice**

**Ice-cold Champagne**

Add a medium-sized rock or a few 1-inch (2.5-cm) ice cubes to a goblet glass. Combine the gin, syrup, and lemon juice in the base of a cocktail shaker. Add a generous quantity of large Ice cubes, close the shaker, and shake vigorously for 15 to 20 seconds. Fine strain over the ice into the goblet glass and top with no more than 2 ounces (60 ml) Champagne. Garnish with an inch-wide (2.5-cm) twist of lemon, slipped in between the rock and the glass. Or, quite cunning, with a freshly plucked pineapple frond, cut to be slightly longer than the height of the glass and anchored between it and the rock.

# Trading Up

One's value on the marriage mart may fluctuate wildly. Gather two mamas in a corner with a titillating tipple, for example, and a suitor who once ranked two dances on a debutante's dance card may suddenly discover she's lost all memory of him entirely! This could prove useful.

**1½ ounces (45 ml) dry vermouth**

**½ ounce (15 ml) Benedictine liqueur**

**½ ounce (15 ml) Drambuie liqueur**

**½ ounce (15 ml) lemon juice**

**Ice-cold Champagne**

Combine the vermouth, liqueurs, and lemon juice in the base of a cocktail shaker. Add a generous quantity of large ice cubes and shake vigorously for 15 to 20 seconds. Fine strain into a coupe, top with Champagne, and garnish—if one so desires. A yellow rose petal would suit this drink perfectly.

Whilst one can never have too much Champagne, when adding the sparkler to a drink, less is more. The correct amount to add is about 1 to 3 ounces (45 to 90 ml), which in a coupe glass will bring one's cocktail to just below the rim. And though Champagne is my particular preference, one may of course use any sparkling wine that one has in one's cellar, such as cava from Spain, prosecco from Italy, or crémant from Burgundy. Most important, one must avoid sweet styles and be sure to select a brut or dry sparkler.

# Sparkling Diadem

Will another Diamond ever make as brilliant a debut as a certain now-duchess? One remembers with great fondness the . . . shall we say, ecstasy? . . . of that scandalous season, as alluring as this sumptuous sparkler.

**1½ ounces (45 ml) Cognac**

**¾ ounce (22.5 ml) pear liqueur**

**¾ ounce (22.5 ml) lemon**

**Ice-cold Champagne**

Combine the Cognac, liqueur, and lemon juice in the base of a cocktail shaker. Add a generous quantity of large ice cubes, close the shaker, and shake vigorously for 15 to 20 seconds. Fine strain into a flute glass, and top with Champagne. If one wishes, garnish with a thin lengthwise-slice of fresh pear, which one should first spritz with a small amount of lemon juice to prevent any discolouration.

If one is so lucky as to have bountiful pear orchards on the grounds of one's country castle, one should immediately set about having bottles of heady pear cordial made from the lushly perfumed produce. One simply layers chopped pears into a jar, sprinkling each layer with several spoonfuls of sugar, then adds a vanilla bean and tops the jar off full of brandy. Set aside someplace dark and relatively warm for several days, until the liqueur becomes slightly syrupy and takes on the pears' floral sweetness and a luscious hint of vanilla. Fine strain through a layer of cheesecloth set into a sieve. This same method works well to make other fruit liqueurs, too.

# Domestic Bliss

These days, a certain energetic young couple is frequently absent from the ballroom. 'Tis a pity for the *ton*! Yet, as one imagines the enticing horizons they are, one hopes, still eagerly exploring, one raises a glass to their fruitful endeavours.

1 ounce (30 ml) Plymouth gin

1 ounce (30 ml) raspberry liqueur

1 ounce (30 ml) ruby red port or fruity red wine

Ice-cold Champagne

In a glass or crystal mixing vessel, gently stir the gin, liqueur, and port with several large rocks of ice until well chilled, about 25 to 30 stirs. Strain into a coupe and top with Champagne. Drop a plump, ripe raspberry into the glass to garnish.

# Unrequited Affection

A dazzling conquest is the toast of the season, but we leave the lovelorn too often to nurse their sorrows in silence—a disaster when strong drink is involved. To whit, the case of the artless young debutante whose longing gaze settles upon her dearest childhood companion—whilst his romantic attention remains elusive, at best. Dear child, bide your time. And your tongue. This toned-down tipple will help.

2 ounces (60 ml) blanc vermouth

¼ ounce (7.5 ml) lemon juice

½ ounce (15 ml) simple syrup (see page 21)

3 dashes lemon bitters

1½ ounces (45 ml) ice-cold Champagne

1½ ounces (45 ml) ice-cold seltzer

In a balloon glass, combine the blanc vermouth, lemon juice, simple syrup, and bitters. Add a large rock or several 1-inch (2.5-cm) ice cubes, then top with the Champagne and seltzer. Garnish with a lemon twist and a single tear.

# Family Jewels

A particularly keen-witted debutante, stepping into society with all the glee of a heretic facing the bonfire, rouses one's deepest sympathy: The genteel domesticity of marriage is hardly likely to satisfy such a gem. In a woman like this, forthright bitterness and disarming effervescence go hand in glove, much as they do in this lively drink.

1 ounce (30 ml) Plymouth gin

1 ounce (30 ml) sweet vermouth

1 ounce (30 ml) green Chartreuse liqueur

1 ounce (30 ml) ice-cold Champagne

In a glass or crystal mixing vessel, gently stir the gin, vermouth, and liqueur with several large rocks of ice until well chilled, about 25 to 30 stirs. Strain into a coupe and top with the Champagne. Garnish with an orange twist and a sigh of solidarity.

# Duty & Desire

Once a preening and pampered eligible heir declares himself finally ready for marriage—much to his mother's delight and the *ton's* collective tizzy—one may next have the joy of watching the wretch mope and whine his way through the rituals of courtship! It's enough to make one wish to drown oneself in this pleasing little cocktail.

Apiphobia has been known since the time of the ancient Greeks, who were the first to document the paralyzing terror of bees. Let it not stand between you and honey syrup, however, as it is an absolute revelation in cocktails. To make it, mix two parts honey to one part boiling water and stir until combined.

1½ ounces (45 ml) gold Barbados rum

¾ ounce (22.5 ml) lime juice

¾ (22.5 ml) ounce honey syrup (see sidebar)

Ice-cold Champagne

Combine the rum, lime juice, and honey syrup in the base of a cocktail shaker. Add a generous quantity of large ice cubes, close the shaker, and shake vigorously for 15 to 20 seconds. Fine strain into a coupe and top with Champagne.

# Glittering Enigma

To be amongst the secret ranks of the *ton*'s subversives is to live a double life—behind closed doors and under cover of darkness, guarded by mystery. This sultry cocktail revels in such unbridled sensations, like those amongst us—no names, of course—who find themselves drawn toward the flames of illicit passion.

**1 ounce (30 ml) bourbon**

**1 ounce (30 ml) sweet vermouth**

**1 ounce (30 ml) ruby red port**

**Dash Angostura bitters**

**Ice-cold Champagne**

In a glass or crystal mixing vessel, gently stir the bourbon, sweet vermouth, port, and bitters with several large rocks of ice until well chilled, about 25 to 30 stirs. Strain into a coupe, top with Champagne, and garnish with a candied cherry.

# Diamond of the Season

There is no corner of London unaware that a young debutante's prospects hinge entirely on our dear queen's approval. But from time to time, when a jewel catches the queen's eye, could there be more than just grace and beauty at play? Perhaps the aftereffects of a particularly enchanting cocktail (rumoured to be Her Majesty's favourite)? One wonders.

**1 barspoon absinthe**

**1½ ounces (45 ml) Plymouth gin**

**¾ ounce (22.5 ml) lemon juice**

**½ ounce (15 ml) simple syrup (see page 21)**

**Ice-cold Champagne**

Dribble the barspoon of absinthe into a flute glass and swirl so the liqueur coats the inside, then pour out the excess. Combine the gin, lemon juice, and simple syrup in the base of a cocktail shaker. Add a generous quantity of large ice cubes, close the shaker, and shake vigorously for 15 to 20 seconds. Fine strain into the flute and top with Champagne to just below the rim of the glass. Garnish as one sees fit—unless, of course, one is serving the queen, in which case a single blush-pink petal is de rigueur.

# Diamond in the Rough

In its infinite wisdom, the *ton* is apt to relegate a sharp-tongued woman to the wallflowers. And yet, a bona fide Fury* is often just what is wanted to take an imperious suitor down a peg or two. When such a pairing comes to pass, it is (usually) a deeply satisfying turn, best toasted with a bright and spicy quaff.

**2 ounces (60 ml) Plymouth navy-strength gin**

**¾ ounce (22.5 ml) lime juice**

**¾ ounce (22.5 ml) Fresh Ginger Syrup (see page 158)**

**1 dash Angostura bitters**

**Ice-cold seltzer**

Fill a highball glass nearly to the top with 1-inch (2.5-cm) ice cubes. Combine the gin, lime juice, ginger syrup, and bitters in the base of a cocktail shaker. Add a medium-sized ice shard, lightly smashed into bits, or 1 or 2 cubes of ice; close the shaker and shake vigorously until the ice is nearly all melted, a technique we call "whipping." Add about 2 ounces (60 ml) seltzer to the shaker, then empty its contents, including any lingering ice, into the glass. If the cocktail doesn't rise nearly to the top of the glass, add no more than an ounce (30 ml) additional seltzer. Garnish with a sprig of fresh mint and, if one has it, a cocktail pick speared with candied ginger.

One makes the most cunning garnish to adorn one's drink by spiking one's garnish with a metal or wooden cocktail pick and placing it in or across one's glass (size the pick appropriately to one's glassware). One can also make a "pin" to grip the side of a glass by spearing two small wooden picks through the garnish side by side, and then scissoring it over the rim.

*Said with the most sincere admiration.

# Cutting Glance

Maneuvering for rank and advantage in the ballroom requires cutthroat composure. Hesitate, and your rival has triumphed. If courage fails as the adversary approaches, turn to this fortifying cocktail and discover one's capacity for subtle annihilation.

**2 ounces (60 ml) rye whiskey**

**½ ounce (15 ml) curaçao**

**2 dashes orange bitters**

**3 dashes aromatic bitters**

**Ice-cold Champagne**

In a glass or crystal mixing vessel, stir the whiskey, curaçao, and orange and aromatic bitters with several large rocks of ice until well chilled, about 25 to 30 stirs. Strain into a coupe and top with Champagne. Garnish with a twisting curl of orange peel.

# Satin Knee Breeches

The prudent provocateur errs on the side of subtlety in all things, including cocktails. When stamina is one's aim (and, reader, when is it not?), look to a nuanced quaff, such as this.

**1 barspoon absinthe**

**2 ounces (60 ml) Plymouth gin**

**¾ ounce (22.5 ml) dry vermouth**

**¾ ounce (22.5 ml) Maraschino liqueur**

**2 dashes orange bitters**

**Ice-cold Champagne**

Drizzle the absinthe into a tall flute glass and swirl so the liqueur coats the inside of the glass, then pour out the excess. Combine the gin, vermouth, liqueur, and bitters in the base of a cocktail shaker, then add a generous quantity of large ice cubes and shake vigorously for 15 to 20 seconds. Fine strain into the flute and top with Champagne. Garnish with two candied cherries, preferably "pinned" to the rim of the glass (see page 46), or a single cherry dropped into the drink.

# Worthy Suitor

The *ton*'s feelings about the rake are more complicated than customarily acknowledged. In public we cheer his rehabilitation, but on the eve of his marriage, we should all pray for his continued debauchery. One hopes domesticity brings a couple both a happy hearth <u>and</u> a raging, unquenchable fire, does one not? Quite like this cocktail, which is smoky, sweet, and utterly unreformed.

1½ ounces (45 ml) peated Scotch whisky

¾ ounce (22.5 ml) Drambuie liqueur

Ice-cold Champagne

Place a single large rock or several 1-inch (2.5-cm) cubes in a rocks glass. Measure and pour the whisky and liqueur over the ice, then with a teaspoon, gently stir the drink 5 or 6 times. Top with Champagne and garnish with a lemon twist.

Whilst on the subject of redeemable men, one should be quite clear that there is a world of difference between the common rake and a rogue or a scoundrel. A rake is careless, but not heartless. Rogues and scoundrels, on the other hand, are not only careless and heartless but merciless to boot. Rakes are rather too much vilified. Rogues and scoundrels, hardly enough.

# Scribbling Woman

Here's a sip as captivating as the quill of the *ton*'s most notorious covert chronicler—and every bit as mysterious. Just two ingredients, yet capable of merciless ruination. Should it find its way to the lips of a rival—or a friend!—who knows what secrets would pour forth?

3-4 ounces (90-120 ml) ice-cold Champagne

¼-½ ounce (7.5-15 ml) absinthe

Pour ice-cold Champagne into a coupe. Add the smaller quantity of absinthe whilst observing the liqueur turn the clear liquid faintly green and opaque. Sip, then add additional absinthe if so emboldened. Garnish with an ounce of bravado.

# Scandalous Rumour

Should one arise wondering if an evening's entertainment has been ranked a success, one need only inquire of one's lady's maid. If that good and indispensable lady has breakfasted on gossip with her tea and toast, fret not: Success is achieved. Should her cheeks blush the hue of this lush tipple, more's the better: It portends a truly torrid tale.

**1 ounce (30 ml) Plymouth gin**

**½ ounce (15 ml) crème de cassis liqueur**

**½ ounce (15 ml) lemon juice**

**2 dashes orange bitters**

**Ice-cold Champagne**

Combine the gin, liqueur, lemon juice, and bitters in the base of a cocktail shaker. Add a generous quantity of large ice cubes, close the shaker, and shake vigorously for 15 to 20 seconds. Fine strain into a flute glass and top with Champagne. Garnish as one desires, perhaps with a juicy blackberry or a hothouse flower, something dewy and tremulous, to be sure.

# Chapter 3

# SOCIAL GRACES

## MASTERING THE ART OF THE PUNCHBOWL

At an evening soirée, whilst the orchestra is still tuning and dance cards are being filled, I set out to find the punchbowl. If there is naught but a lemonade table—and not even a very good one at that—I tell the footmen to keep my carriage close: The fun will have to be had elsewhere. But if the punch is well appointed and the punchbowl already drawing a crowd, there's a good chance we shall all be dancing until the sunrise.

The punchbowl, reader, is an extension of the dance floor. Spinning through a quadrille, one locks eyes and feels the gentle touch of several different partners. It is intoxicating! And when the dance is done, to be guided to the punchbowl—fingers interlocked through thin gloves, the heat of a partner's hand at the small of one's back—is to be taken to an intimate sanctum, a crowd composed almost entirely of conspiring couples. Whilst a suitor whispers bon mots in a debutante's ear, at her elbow her mama may be plotting her marriage to another!

If the punch itself is too spirited, however, inflamed emotions peak too quickly and one's glittering gala—not to mention one's possible love match—becomes a spoiled, sodden affair. If it is too weak, on the other hand, the courage for mischief goes lacking. A good punch is a carefully calibrated cocktail skillfully crafted in large quantities, as stimulating as it is refreshing, but never quite over the top. A ditty from Barbados, birthplace of punch, is helpful to remember the traditional formulation:

"One of sour, two of sweet, three of strong, and four of weak."

Master the punchbowl, and one's invitation will be sought as eagerly as a six-figure dowry. Just remember, keep the bowl well chilled and well filled at all times. It is the evening's oracle: As goes the punch, so goes the party.

## INTERLUDE
# On Charm & Chilling

One's punch will quickly become a flavoured water if one uses the incorrect ice, as the rocks and cubes used for cocktails melt too quickly in the punchbowl, diluting the concoction. Instead, one should prepare a decorative ice ring or block. One goes about it thusly:

## 1.
Select the ice-molding form. Pans for making cakes are exemplary, in particular if they are ornately shaped. Ensure the form fits inside one's punchbowl.

## 2.
Prepare one's garnishes. Sliced or whole fruits for a fruited punch, for example, or cinnamon sticks, cloves, and star anise for a spiced brew. One can also freeze sliced citrus, herb sprigs, and flowers, leaves, and petals.

## 3.
Freeze in layers. First, arrange the bottom layer of garnishes—which will appear atop the floating ice ring—leaving space between the elements so each individual garnish can be admired. Add just enough water to anchor the layer in place when frozen, then freeze until set, about 2 hours. Repeat approximately three times, until the form is filled nearly to the brim.

## 4.
Freeze entirely. One's ice mold should be crafted at least 24 hours before it is required.

## 5.
Unmold. To release the ice from its form, dip the pan into hot water, then invert and slip the molded ice into the punch.

# Genteel Curtsy

SERVES 8 TO 10

If one arrives at a fete on the arm of a male chaperone, one should endeavour to extricate herself from his company as quickly as possible. A hovering mama is one thing. An overzealous brother is a different disaster entirely. Send him to fetch you a glass of this punch: Its demure appearance raises no cause for fraternal alarm.

18 ounces (540 ml) Cognac

3 ounces (90 ml) Heering cherry liqueur

6 ounces (180 ml) lemon juice

Handful of raspberries

1½ (750-ml) bottles rosé, chilled

Combine the Cognac, liqueur, and lemon juice in a vessel and chill for at least 3 hours, but no longer than 8. When it's time to set out the punchbowl, add the chilled Cognac mixture to the bowl along with the berries. Pour the chilled wine over the top and float an ice ring in the bowl (see page 57).

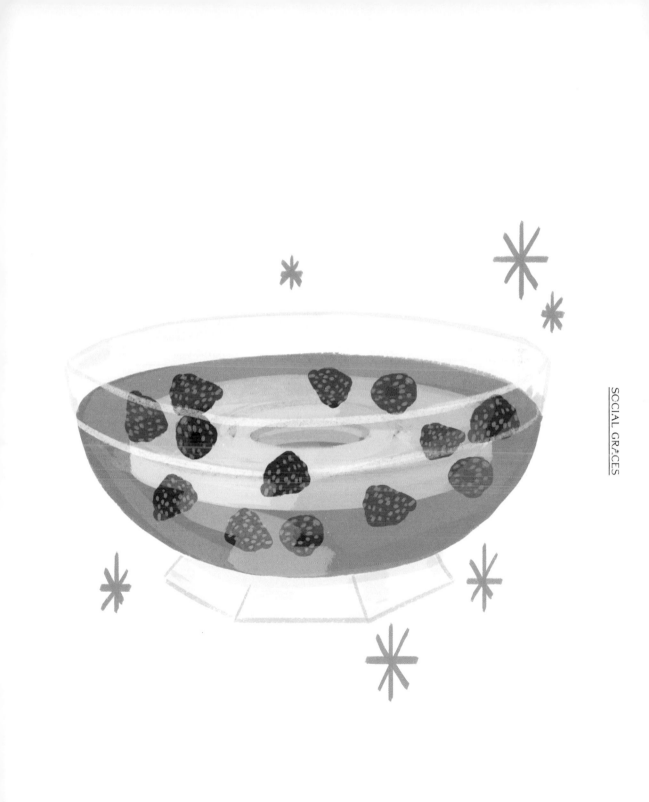

# Accomplished Swoon

SERVES 10 TO 12

When deployed precisely at the pivotal moment, the debutante's prerogative to wither elegantly is amongst her most impressive stratagems. Revived with a cup of this delicate refreshment, she is catapulted to the highest ranks of fascination, a most opportune perch from which to command a dithering suitor.

10 ounces (300 ml) gin

4 ounces (120 ml) Fresh Raspberry Syrup (see page 157)

6 ounces (180 ml) lemon juice

1 teaspoon rose water

36-40 ounces (1-1.2 L) ice-cold seltzer

Combine the gin, syrup, lemon juice, and rose water in a vessel and chill for at least 3 hours, but no longer than 8. When it's time to set out the punchbowl, add the chilled gin mixture to the bowl, float an ice ring (see page 57) or block in the bowl, and pour the chilled seltzer over the top, adjusting the quantity for desired strength and taste.

Rose water's perfume can be shockingly bellicose. Start with this restrained amount, and if, after one has added the seltzer, one feels one's punch is lacking sufficient floral fragrance, add additional rose water in increments of 1 teaspoon, until one's desired bouquet is achieved.

# First Waltz

SERVES 6 TO 8

Bewitching as this brew may be, be wary, lest under its influence one take too many turns about the dance floor with an unsuitable suitor—no matter how dashing. One dance is a flirtation. Two is a romance. Three is a lifetime of penance paid for impropriety.

16 ounces (480 ml)
Jamaican rum

8 ounces (240 ml)
grapefruit juice

8 ounces (240 ml)
orange juice

4 ounces (120 ml)
lemon juice

3 ounces (90 ml)
Maraschino liqueur

1½-2 ounces (45-60 ml)
simple syrup
(see page 21)

1½ ounces (45 ml)
allspice dram

Angostura bitters

Combine the rum, juices, liqueur, syrup, and allspice dram in a vessel; add bitters to taste (and more syrup to sweeten the punch, if necessary), and chill for at least 3 hours, but no longer than 8. When it's time to set out the punchbowl, add the chilled rum mixture to the bowl and float an ice ring (see page 57) or block in the bowl. It is a potent punch and should be served on ice: Set out additional 1-inch (2.5-cm) cubes in a Champagne bucket, to be added to one's cup.

A ship captain occasionally sails into my port bearing gifts from around the globe. A recent offering was this allspice dram, a rum liqueur, brought from the island of Jamaica. It's flavoured with a fruit we English call "allspice," though it's actually the berry of the pimento tree. It's a rather literal name, as the pimento fruit tastes of clove, cinnamon, and nutmeg combined. Hardly "all" the spices, but there one is.

Dances
1. Waltz - - - - - - -
2. Waltz - - - - - - -
3. Waltz - - - - - - - - -
4. Polka - - - - - - - - -
5. Waltz - - - - - - - -
6. Waltz - - - - - - - -
7. Waltz - - - - - - - -
8. Lancers - - - - - - -
9. Waltz - - - -

Can a public twirl be as thrilling as a private assignation? Indeed, yes, reader, if a debutante is daring enough to grasp the opportunity. Practice one's submissive countenance—the *ton* is blind to wickedness masked by the face of an angel. And when the orchestra ceases, promptly excuse oneself to the punchbowl for a cup of this innocent quaff.

**5 ounces (150 ml) Plymouth gin**

**4 ounces (120 ml) sweet vermouth**

**2 ounces (60 ml) tawny port**

**1¾ ounces (52.5 ml) curaçao**

**6 ounces (180 ml) simple syrup (see page 21)**

**8 ounces (240 ml) lemon juice**

**1 quart (960 ml) ice-cold seltzer**

**5–6 sprigs mint, tender tips only**

**¼ cucumber, cut crosswise into thin slices**

**¼ orange, sliced into wheels**

**¼ lemon, sliced into wheels**

**3–4 strawberries, sliced into quarters**

Combine the gin, vermouth, port, curaçao, syrup, and lemon juice in a vessel and chill for at least 3 hours, but no longer than 8. When it's time to set out the punchbowl, add the chilled mixture to the bowl along with the seltzer, mint, cucumbers, citrus, and strawberries. Float an ice ring in the bowl (see page 57).

# Hunting Fortunes

**SERVES 6 TO 8**

Here's a punch that does not disguise its ambitions, unlike the suitor cloaked in velvet, brocade, and questionable sincerity. Reader, assume that a glib gentleman's tongue is an instrument of duplicity and focus instead on his eyes. If they glitter avariciously, enjoy the flattery, but exile his name from your dance card.

16 ounces (480 ml) Irish whiskey

16 ounces (480 ml) strongly brewed black tea, cooled

4 ounces (120 ml) lemon juice

6 ounces (180 ml) orange juice

4 ounces (120 ml) oleo saccharum (see page 66)

4–6 dashes Angostura bitters

3 cups (720 ml) ice-cold water

Freshly grated nutmeg

Combine the whiskey, tea, juices, oleo saccharum, and bitters to taste in a vessel and chill for at least 3 hours, but no longer than 8. When it's time to set out the punchbowl, add the chilled whiskey mixture to the bowl, add the water, and float an ice ring in the bowl (see page 57). Grate a generous amount of fresh nutmeg over the top.

# Terrifying Dowager

SERVES 12

When the dance floor parts like the sea in a biblical exodus, one can be confident a certain intimidating grande dame is approaching. And that in her regal wake, the punchbowl will be thronged by gentlemen nursing their collective backbone with a draught of this edifying concoction.

8 ounces (240 ml) Cognac

12 ounces (360 ml) oloroso sherry

12 ounces (360 ml) gold Barbados rum

12 ounces (360 ml) dry red wine

4 ounces (120 ml) oleo saccharum (see below)

16 ounces (480 ml) strongly brewed black tea, cooled

4 ounces (120 ml) lemon juice

12 ounces (360 ml) ice-cold Champagne

Combine the Cognac, sherry, rum, wine, oleo saccharum, tea, and lemon juice in a vessel and chill for at least 3 hours, but no longer than 8. When it's time to set out the punchbowl, add the chilled mixture to the bowl, pour the Champagne over the top, and float an ice ring in the bowl (see page 57).

Oleo saccharum, a syrup of citrus oils and sugar, is elemental to good punch. To make it, carefully peel the skin from 4 lemons and 4 oranges, avoiding the white pith. Muddle these in a bowl with ½ cup (100 g) sugar, and set aside for at least 3 hours and up to one day: It will become quite syrupy. Strain, pressing on the skins. This will make about 4 ounces (120 ml) syrup, enough for a bowl of punch.

# Incorrigible Gossip

### SERVES 10 TO 12

When punch and pique are combined, beware the vengeful debutante. After a glass or two of this stimulating tipple, one vanquished rival still bandies about salacious stories regarding a certain couple whom she claims she spied in a passionate embrace—on the eve of their engagement. Reader, as sordid tales go, that one is sorely lacking, given the happy ending. But the moral remains: Underestimate the spitefulness of the spurned at one's peril.

3 ounces (90 ml) Cognac

4 ounces (120 ml) Pusser's rum

1 ounce (30 ml) Maraschino liqueur

3-4 ounces (90-120 ml) oleo saccharum (see page 66)

16 ounces (480 ml) brewed green tea, cooled

8 ounces (240 ml) pineapple juice

1 (750-ml) bottle ice-cold Champagne

Combine the Cognac, rum, liqueur, 3 ounces (90 ml) of the oleo saccharum, green tea, and pineapple juice in a vessel, taste and adjust the sweetness by adding more oleo saccharum, if necessary, and chill for at least 3 hours, but no longer than 8. When it's time to set out the punchbowl, add the chilled mixture to the bowl, pour the Champagne over the top, and float an ice ring in the bowl (see page 57).

# Shock and Delight

## SERVES 10 TO 12

Notorious for its capacity to spur lapses in both judgment and inhibition, this bittersweet sip is often served when Her Majesty is expected in attendance. She has been noted to request a seat as near as possible to any large potted palms, or an unlighted gallery, or dim balcony, though one is uncertain whether her quarry be careless couples or covert gossips.

**24 ounces (720 ml) oloroso sherry**

**12 ounces (360 ml) blanc vermouth**

**4–6 dashes Angostura bitters**

**1 quart (960 ml) ice-cold tonic water**

Combine the sherry, vermouth, and bitters to taste in a vessel and chill for at least 3 hours, but no longer than 8. When it's time to set out the punchbowl, add the chilled sherry mixture to the bowl, pour the chilled tonic water over the top, and float an ice ring in the bowl (see page 57).

In India, to combat mosquito-borne fevers, our officers take a tasty tonic mixed with sugar, sparkling water, and medicinal quinine derived from the bark of the South American cinchona tree. Having captured our queen's fancy, the bitter brew is likely to soon become quite fashionable.

# Wayward Touch

SERVES 12

In the arms of a handsome suitor twirling about the dance floor, one's thirst can grow unbearable. Moderate one's indulgence! The last time this quenching quaff was served at a ball, no fewer than three elopements followed.

18 ounces (540 ml) Cognac

18 ounces (540 ml) pear liqueur

12 ounces (360 ml) lemon juice

9 ounces (265 ml) curaçao

6 ounces (180 ml) Cinnamon Syrup (see page 157)

18 ounces (540 ml) ice-cold Champagne

Combine the Cognac, liqueur, lemon juice, curaçao, and syrup in a vessel and chill for at least 3 hours, but no longer than 8. When it's time to set out the punchbowl, add the chilled Cognac mixture to the bowl, pour the chilled Champagne over the top, and float an ice ring in the bowl (see page 57).

# Dancing Partner

SERVES 10 TO 12

If a love match is truly one's aim, one should pay less heed to the polished suitors circling the Diamonds of the first water, and more to the gentleman fetching a parched wallflower a cup of this light and fizzy tipple, no matter his rank or comeliness. He may well be the catch of the season.

16 ounces (480 ml) Manzanilla or fino sherry

8 ounces (240 ml) lemon juice

6 ounces (180 ml) Cinnamon Syrup (page 157)

2 ounces (60 ml) simple syrup (see page 21)

30 ounces (880 ml) ice-cold seltzer

Combine the sherry, lemon juice, and syrups in a vessel and chill for at least 3 hours, but no longer than 8. When it's time to set out the punchbowl, add the chilled sherry mixture, pour the seltzer over the top, and float an ice ring in the bowl (see page 57).

# Brazen Matchmaker

## SERVES 12

A nervous mama is apt to plunge one too quickly into a shallow pool of prospects. Before alighting on the dance floor, settle her into a quiet corner—alone!—with a cup of this soothing remedy.

**20 ounces (600 ml) Manzanilla sherry**

**10 ounces (300 ml) Carpano Antica sweet vermouth**

**18 ounces (540 ml) strongly brewed black tea, cooled**

**6 ounces (180 ml) lemon juice**

**6 ounces (180 ml) simple syrup (see page 21)**

**16 ounces (480 ml) ice-cold Champagne**

Combine the sherry, vermouth, tea, lemon juice, and syrup in a vessel and chill for at least 3 hours, but no longer than 8. When it's time to set out the punchbowl, add the chilled sherry mixture, pour the Champagne over the top, and float an ice ring in the bowl (see page 57).

Should one happen to find oneself sipping vermouth with the Duke of Savoy, one will be tasting Carpano Antica, the official court quaff, quite luscious and full bodied compared to other sweet vermouths. It tastes strongly of vanilla, orange peel, and dried cherries, with a little cacao nib bitterness.

# Debutante's Ruin

## SERVES 6 TO 8

Though a coterie of the *ton*'s gossips will assure one of scorn
and perpetual social damnation, if one trusts the fealty of one's
partner implicitly—follow one's heart! Take two cups
of this seductive quaff to the darkened terrace and commence
one's lascivious education.

**16 ounces (480 ml)
Pusser's rum**

**4 ounces (120 ml)
tawny port**

**4 ounces (120 ml)
curaçao**

**4 ounces (120 ml)
falernum liqueur**

**8 ounces (240 ml)
lime juice**

**4 ounces (120 ml)
simple syrup (see
page 21)**

**6–8 dashes Angostura
bitters**

Combine the rum, port, curaçao, liqueur, juice,
syrup, and bitters to taste in a vessel and chill
for at least 3 hours, but no longer than 8. When
it's time to set out the punchbowl, add the
chilled rum mixture and float an ice ring in the
bowl (see page 57). Without extra ice in one's
cup, this punch may prove more potent than one
finds pleasant. Set out additional 1-inch (2.5-cm)
cubes of ice in a Champagne bucket.

I have a dashing young naval officer to thank for my introduction to falernum,
another Caribbean liqueur, this one from the island of Barbados. It is a punch-like
cordial of lime, rum, sugar, and spices; the exact recipe is a closely held secret.

# Chapter 4

## DELICATE DAYTIME DRINKS

### REFRESHING, LOWER-POTENCY LIBATIONS

I once caused a (very) minor scandal by refusing to appear in my mama's drawing room, or any drawing room, for the length of an entire season. It was a fledgling form of protest. One that, with time and distance, I am inclined to view more with humour than regret. The drawing room can be <u>exceptionally</u> dull. There is a reason its furnishings are usually upright and straight backed: to discourage sleep.

But now that I am no longer expected to perform in the drawing room like a trained monkey—and have fully embraced its gossip-liberating potential—I feel somewhat more kindly toward the space. And besides, I have decided to follow my own counsel regarding daytime decorum. I serve drinks.

Not every cocktail is suited to the purpose, of course. Inebriation under gentle cover of darkness can be acquitted as excessive gaiety. By day, it is very likely ruinous.

Thus the typical daytime cocktail is far less brawny, substituting aromatic fortified wine in place of all or most of the strong spirit. And yet daytime drinks are no less invigorating, as witnessed by one's newfound tolerance for eccentric poets and amateur sopranos. Better still, many are served fizzy and icy cold. When I press a frosted glass into a weary debutante's hand and sense her immediate revivification, I brim with satisfaction.

With planning, one can transport the daytime tipple out of doors and enjoy its effects without compromising one's ability to play lawn games, or admire a garden walk, or make witty conversation. Indeed, one may even find these skills enhanced. At minimum, there is generally a pleasant readiness to enjoy small talk about the weather, an ability which normally takes one several seasons to cultivate.

*You are welcome*

Since making their way from Geneva to London, Mr. Schweppe's sparkling seltzer waters have been employed primarily to remedy ailments of the stomach. However, their consummate purpose is to enliven cocktails. When making a fizzy drink, one preserves the strength of its spirits by shaking and chilling the ingredients of the core cocktail with but a scant amount of ice, a technique called "whipping." One then tops the drink with chilled seltzer and serves the drink as cold as possible over yet more ice. The refreshment is perfectly sublime.

# Dear Mama

One Grosvenor Square matriarch possesses several of the most enviable elements of drawing room décor: handsome eligible sons. Yet even without their lanky frames draped over the plush powder-blue settees, an invitation to take tea with the doyenne is eagerly pursued by the ladies of the *ton*. Perhaps because, under the right circumstances, the madame has been known to offer this refined tipple?

1¾ ounces (52.5 ml) Manzanilla sherry

1 ounce (30 ml) dry vermouth

¼ ounce (7.5 ml) Maraschino liqueur

1 dash orange bitters

1 dash lemon bitters

In a glass or crystal mixing vessel, gently stir the sherry, vermouth, liqueur, and bitters with several large rocks of ice until well chilled, about 25 to 30 stirs. Strain into a coupe and garnish with an orange twist and a candied cherry.

# Cherished Companion

Not even rainbow-hued frocks will render a drawing room less gray and dreary when scandal and tragedy drape a household in woe and mourning. Should such a calamity come to pass (reader, one must be <u>ever</u> prepared), take solace in heartfelt friendship and this revitalizing sip, irrepressible as a ray of sunshine.

1 ounce (30 ml) Plymouth navy-strength gin

1 ounce (30 ml) sweet vermouth

¾ ounce (22.5 ml) lemon juice

½ ounce (15 ml) Fresh Ginger Syrup (see page 158)

¼ ounce (7.5 ml) simple syrup (see page 21)

2 strawberries, sliced

3 slices fresh cucumber

Ice-cold seltzer

Fill a balloon glass about two-thirds full of rocks cracked from a solid ice block or 1-inch (2.5-cm) ice cubes. Combine the gin, vermouth, lemon juice, syrups, strawberries, and cucumber in the base of a cocktail shaker and lightly muddle. Add a generous quantity of large ice cubes, close the shaker, and shake vigorously for 15 to 20 seconds. Add 2 to 3 ounces (60 to 90 ml) of seltzer to the shaker, then fine strain the cocktail into the glass. Garnish, perhaps, with a flower or a fresh strawberry and slices of cucumber; or at least with one's unwavering moral support.

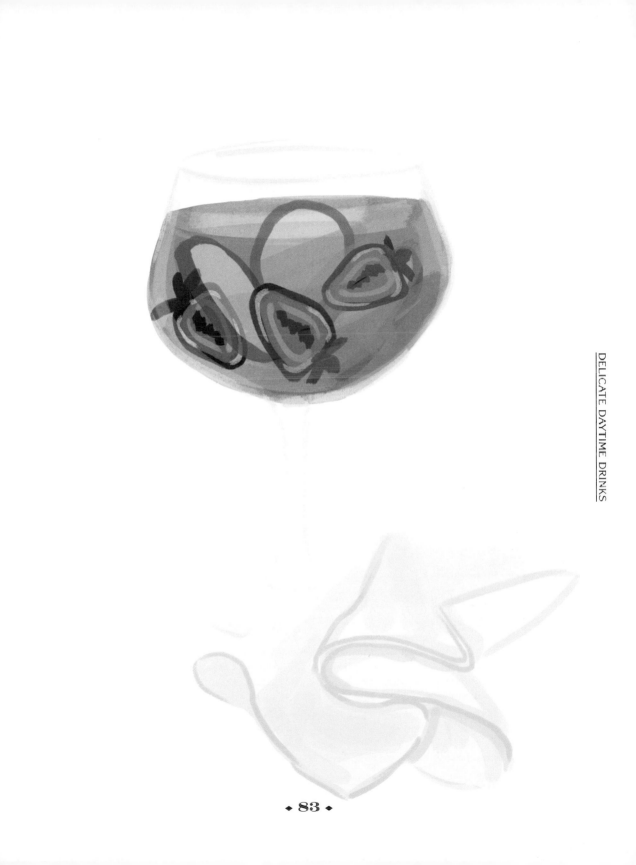

# Advantageous Match

The ballroom is for fantasy and flirtation. One faces the brass tacks of the marriage mart in the drawing room. Should a suitor fail to make his expected appearance—or worse, appear, but utterly devoid of his evening luster—I offer this sweet sip, a balm for one's bruised sensibilities.

2 ounces (60 ml) Madeira

1 ounce (30 ml) lime juice

½ ounce (15 ml) simple syrup (see page 21)

3 strawberries, sliced

Combine the Madeira, lime juice, simple syrup, and strawberries in the base of a cocktail shaker and lightly muddle until the fruit is gently bruised, but not squished. Add a generous quantity of large ice cubes, close the shaker, and shake vigorously for 15 to 20 seconds. Fine strain into a coupe. Float a sympathetic flower, like a teensy tiny daisy, or sprinkling of forlorn petals across the drink's surface.

In drink making, "muddling" refers not to the botching of one's personal affairs but to the act of infusing spirits with bruised fruit or herbs, and is done with a wooden dowel, like an apothecary pestle. Alternately, one can skip the muddling and use the ice itself to pulverize the fruit or herbs during the shake. Either technique will suffice. Muddling can be cathartic when one is feeling nettled.

# Carriage Ride

Five minutes alone in the drawing room with a man will heap scandal on a young debutante. Yet, curiously, the *ton* thinks nothing of an unchaperoned dash about the park in the gentleman's curricle. Consider it a loophole, reader, and make haste. The taste of freedom is as scrumptious as this fizzy and full-bodied quaff.

1 ounce (30 ml) falernum liqueur

1 ounce (30 ml) Carpano Antica sweet vermouth

½ ounce (15 ml) Manzanilla sherry

¾ ounce (22.5 ml) lime juice

Ice-cold seltzer

Fill a highball glass nearly to the top with rocks cracked from a solid ice block, or 1-inch (2.5-cm) ice cubes, or a frozen spear of ice (see page 22). Combine the liqueur, vermouth, sherry, and lime juice in the base of a cocktail shaker. Add a medium-sized ice shard, lightly smashed into bits, or one or two cubes of ice; close the shaker and shake vigorously until the ice is nearly all melted—this is "whipping." Add about 2 ounces (60 ml) seltzer to the shaker, then empty its contents, including any lingering ice, into the highball glass. If the cocktail doesn't rise nearly to the glass rim, add no more than about an ounce (30 ml) of additional seltzer. Garnish with a lime wedge or wheel.

# Country Seat

This delightful drink pulls double duty—a cocktail <u>and</u> a fortifying bit of sustenance, all in one. Just the thing to assist in one's recuperation, after the sorts of intimate al fresco exertions that leave one weak-kneed and trembling.

**2 ounces (60 ml) Manzanilla or fino sherry**

**¾ ounce (22.5 ml) green Chartreuse liqueur**

**1 orange wedge**

**3–4 mixed berries**

**½ ounce (15 ml) lemon juice**

Add the sherry and liqueur to the base of a cocktail shaker. Add the orange wedge and coarsely smash using a muddler, then add the berries and lightly bruise them. Add the lemon juice and swirl. Fill a highball glass about two-thirds full with crushed ice (see page 88), pour the cocktail on top—including all the fruit—then pile with more crushed ice, leaving just enough room in the glass to garnish with a straw, several more fresh berries, an orange twist, and a sprig of mint. One sets oneself apart from one's fellow cocktail makers if one also sprinkles a very light dusting of powdered sugar over the top of the drink.

By no means make this drink with anything other than crushed ice, which is extremely simple and satisfying to make for oneself. To do so, place several hefty shards picked from a solid block of ice, or several 1- to 2-inch (2.5- to 5-cm) cubes, in the center of a clean kitchen cloth. Bring the ends of the cloth up and twist to make a pouch, then hammer it with a heavy metal or wooden mallet. One should periodically lift up the pouch and shake it to loosen the cubes, then hammer again until the largest ice is in bits the size of small stones. Remember, crushed ice melts quickly, so once you have commenced, proceed with all due haste to finish the making of one's cocktail.

# Distant Cousin

Estranged relations make for the most titillating tattle, especially when wills, schemes, and matrimonial machinations are involved. Should such a situation present itself—and, reader, in the *ton* it is only ever a matter of time—serve this faintly spicy concoction, and witness the speculation in one's drawing room scale to astonishing heights.

**1½ ounces (45 ml) Manzanilla sherry**

**1½ ounces (45 ml) sweet vermouth**

**2 dashes orange bitters**

In a glass or crystal mixing vessel, gently stir the sherry, sweet vermouth, and bitters with several large rocks of ice until well chilled, about 25 to 30 stirs. Strain into a coupe and garnish with a lemon twist.

Depending on one's choice of sweet vermouth, the character of this drink can change dramatically. My choice is the French-style sweet vermouth of Mr. Dolin, which is light and soft, and tastes of citrus, spice, and herbs. An Italian-style sweet vermouth will add jammier, more fruity flavours. Also quite delightful! One should experiment.

# Garden Promenade

In the prying eyes of the *ton*, no couple is official until they have appeared arm in arm on a garden path and survived the scrutiny of a certain omniscient gossip columnist. Daunting! But no match for the serene equanimity bestowed by this pleasantly cooling quaff.

**Small handful mint**

**1 ounce (30 ml) Plymouth gin**

**1 ounce (30 ml) dry vermouth**

**1 ounce (30 ml) lime juice**

**¾ ounce (22.5 ml) simple syrup (see page 21)**

**Dash celery bitters**

**Ice-cold seltzer**

Place the mint, gin, vermouth, lime, and simple syrup in the bottom of a highball glass and lightly muddle to gently bruise the mint. Fill the glass with crushed ice (see page 88), anchoring the mint leaves to the bottom of the glass, then top with about 2 ounces (60 ml) seltzer, or no more than about 3 ounces (90 ml) if the drink doesn't rise nearly to the rim. Dash with bitters and garnish with another fresh sprig of mint and a wedge or a wheel of lime.

How much mint is a small handful? About six leaves. And when muddling mint, one must always pluck the individual leaves from the stem. Stems in one's drink are a travesty.

# Composition for Pianoforte

In an unguarded moment, a previously tightly wound debutante of no particular virtuosity is thought to have confided to her lady's maid the secret of her newfound placidity and . . . musical dexterity. She said she practiced alone. At night. For pleasure. Not surprisingly, the story traveled through the *ton*'s kitchens and drawing rooms as quickly as this blushing cocktail disappears. There has been a refreshing uptick in debutante talent ever since.

**2 ounces (60 ml) Madeira**

**½ ounce (15 ml) curaçao**

**1½ ounces (45 ml) grapefruit juice**

**¼ ounce (7.5 ml) lemon juice**

**1 barspoon absinthe**

**Ice-cold seltzer**

This drink is delightful garnished with an ample twist of grapefruit peel or a thin round grapefruit wheel, either of which one should position decoratively in a highball glass before filling it nearly to the top with rocks cracked from a solid ice block, or 1-inch (2.5-cm) ice cubes, or a frozen spear of ice (see page 22). Combine the Madeira, curaçao, grapefruit juice, lemon juice, and absinthe in the base of a cocktail shaker. Add a medium-sized ice shard, lightly smashed into bits, or one or two cubes of ice; close the shaker and whip until the ice is nearly all melted. Add about 2 ounces (60 ml) seltzer to the shaker, then empty its contents, including any lingering ice, into the glass. If the cocktail doesn't rise nearly to the glass rim, add no more than about an ounce (30 ml) of additional seltzer.

# Lady's Maid

From the outer fringes of the *ton*, one hears <u>horrifying</u> tales of a beautiful but ill-treated illegitimate daughter, forced to labour in servitude in her own household. Should she escape the grip of her venomous captor, one imagines the mystery woman could become quite the disruptive force. Much like this invigorating drink.

1 ounce (30 ml) Manzanilla sherry

1 ounce (30 ml) Old Tom gin

1 ounce (30 ml) lime juice

¾ ounce (22.5 ml) simple syrup (see page 21)

3 slices fresh cucumber

Small handful mint

Place a large rock or several 1-inch (2.5-cm) cubes in a rocks glass. Combine the sherry, gin, lime juice, simple syrup, cucumber, and mint in the base of a cocktail shaker and lightly muddle. Add a generous quantity of large ice cubes, close the shaker, and shake vigorously for 15 to 20 seconds. Fine strain over ice into the rocks glass. Whilst a simple sprig of mint or a beautiful blossom is a fine garnish for this drink, should one so feel the need, one may take two wooden picks, spear them through a pair of cucumber slices, stab the cucumber with a mint sprig stem, and then scissor the entire garnish onto the rim of the glass. Of course, if one were a man, capable* of actually ridding the world of its domestic injustices, one wouldn't need to exorcise their frustrations upon innocent vegetables.

*In theory.

# Family Picnic

The airy brookside pavilion of a certain tight-knit family is a coveted invitation when the *ton* decamps to the park in fine weather. To find a place beneath its billowing shade is to float in the first water. Plus, the family serves its own signature cocktail, a very first-water indulgence.

**FOR ONE:**

2½ ounces (75 ml) blanc vermouth

¾ ounce (22.5 ml) lime juice

½ ounce (15 ml) Benedictine liqueur

2–3 dashes Angostura bitters

**FOR FIVE:**

12½ ounces (370 ml) blanc vermouth

3¾ ounces (112 ml) lime juice

2½ ounces (75 ml) Benedictine liqueur

5 ounces (150 ml) cold water

Bitters to taste

For a single cocktail, place a large rock or several 1-inch (2.5-cm) cubes in a rocks glass. Combine the vermouth, lime juice, and liqueur in the base of a cocktail shaker. Add a generous quantity of large ice cubes, close the shaker, and shake vigorously for 15 to 20 seconds. Fine strain over ice into the rocks glass then dash with bitters. Garnish with a lime wedge or wheel. To make a bigger batch, combine the vermouth, lime juice, liqueur, and cold water in a vessel and chill until ready to serve, then pour, add bitters to taste to each glass, and garnish.

Should one aspire to their own signature picnic drink, look to recipes for shaken drinks served on the rocks—they are simply prepared in batches for a crowd. An empty wine or spirits bottle will hold about five batches of most shaken cocktail recipes. Thusly, for each bottle, one multiplies each ingredient by five—with the exception of bitters (bring the bitters bottle and add bitters to each glass to taste)—then adds an additional 5 ounces (150 ml) chilled water to the mix, accounting for the dilution one would normally add to the drink whilst shaking (equal to 1 ounce/30 ml per drink). Chill thoroughly, and keep the batched bottled cocktail as cold as possible until the very moment it's poured out on the rocks. Garnish, serve, and enjoy one's budding eminence.

# Kindred Spirit

There is nothing better than having one's expectations turned on their head. Except, perhaps, having them turned on their head by a man whom one has written off as an incorrigible, idiotic egoist— who then shows up in one's drawing room and turns out to be rather handsome and even (possibly) humane. It produces a bitter-sweet, fizzy feeling\*, much like this drink.

1 ounce (30 ml)
Plymouth gin

1 ounce (30 ml)
Salers aperitif liqueur

1½ ounces (45 ml)
grapefruit juice

½ ounce (15 ml)
lemon juice

½ ounce (15 ml)
simple syrup
(see page 21)

Ice-cold seltzer

Fill a highball glass nearly to the top with rocks cracked from a solid ice block, or 1-inch (2.5-cm) ice cubes, or a frozen spear of ice (see page 22). Combine the gin, aperitif, grapefruit juice, lemon juice, and simple syrup in the base of a cocktail shaker. Add a medium-sized ice shard, lightly smashed into bits, or one or two cubes of ice; close the shaker and whip until the ice is nearly all melted. Add about 2 ounces (60 ml) seltzer to the shaker, then empty its contents, including any lingering ice, into the glass. If the cocktail doesn't rise nearly to the glass rim, add no more than about an ounce (30 ml) additional seltzer. For a garnish, one could do no better than a single pale-pink rose petal, though any bloom will complement this lovely drink's delicate blush hue.

Whilst taking the waters amidst the mountain peaks of the French Auvergne, I was given gentian cordials as a medicament and knew immediately that I must try the bitter liqueur in cocktails. Of these, Salers Aperitif La Bounoux Gentiane Liqueur is, as the French say, typique, with a very clean and bright flavor. If one cannot find it, one may substitute another bitter aperitif, preferably French and made from the gentian plant. Italian bitter liqueurs—all of which are divine, each in their own way—are often darker, earthier, and spicier. Let color be your guide: The darker the liqueur's hue, the less like Salers it is likely to taste.

\*Of course, whether that feeling should be trusted or not is another matter entirely.

# Hyde Park

Here's a sweet, spicy, rather smoldering quaff, as rambunctious as
a cavorting canine let loose upon the lanes of Rotten Row—
incidentally a sight seldom seen, given the *ton*'s general disdain
for any hound larger than a lazy lapdog (whilst in London, that is).
What an intriguing opportunity for mayhem. . . .

¼ ounce (7.5 ml)
peated Scotch

1 ounce (30 ml)
Madeira

1 ounce (30 ml)
Manzanilla or fino
sherry

¾ ounce (22.5 ml)
lime juice

½ ounce (15 ml)
falernum liqueur

½ ounce (15 ml)
Fresh Ginger Syrup
(see page 158)

Ice-cold seltzer

Fill a balloon glass about two-thirds full of
crushed ice (see page 88). Combine the Scotch,
Madeira, sherry, lime juice, liqueur, and ginger
syrup in the base of a cocktail shaker. Add a
medium-sized ice shard, lightly smashed into bits,
or one or two cubes of ice; close the shaker and
whip until the ice is nearly all melted. Add about
2 ounces (60 ml) seltzer to the shaker, then
empty its contents, including any lingering ice,
into the glass and garnish with a lime wedge.

# House Party

When one is ensconced in the country for a week or weekend of games and frivolity (see my further thoughts regarding this matter on page 106), one must pace one's indulgences. For refreshment, look to a light and somewhat innocent tipple, such as this.

¾ ounce (22.5 ml)
Old Tom gin

1¼ ounces (37.5 ml)
blanc vermouth

1 ounce (30 ml)
Honey-Tea Syrup
(see page 158)

¾ ounce (22.5 ml)
lemon juice

Ice-cold seltzer

Place two thinly sliced lemon wheels inside a highball glass, then fill nearly to the top with rocks cracked from a solid ice block, or 1-inch (2.5-cm) ice cubes, or a frozen spear of ice (see page 22), anchoring the wheels into place. Combine the gin, vermouth, syrup, and lemon juice in the base of a cocktail shaker. Add a medium-sized ice shard, lightly smashed into bits, or one or two cubes of ice; close the shaker and whip until the ice is nearly all melted. Add about 2 ounces (60 ml) seltzer to the shaker, then empty its contents, including any lingering ice, into the glass. If the cocktail doesn't rise nearly to the glass rim, add no more than about an ounce (30 ml) of additional seltzer.

# Lucky Mallet

A certain songbird recently flown from the city was occasionally loose-lipped on the subject of her former protector. Thus one's knowledge of her pet name for that rogue's, shall we say, favourite piece of sporting equipment. He's known to play particularly ~~well~~ fine after downing a few of these invigorating drinks.

1½ ounces (45 ml) Madeira

1 ounce (30 ml) curaçao

½ ounce (15 ml) simple syrup (see page 21)

¾ ounce (22.5 ml) lemon juice

Rub a lemon wedge around one-half of the outer rim of a rocks glass, then invert the glass into a dish of coarse salt. Place a large rock or several 1-inch (2.5-cm) cubes in the glass. Combine the Madeira, curaçao, syrup, and lemon juice in the base of a cocktail shaker. Add a generous quantity of large ice cubes, close the shaker, and shake vigorously for 15 to 20 seconds. Fine strain over ice into the rocks glass, being careful not to disturb the salt rim.

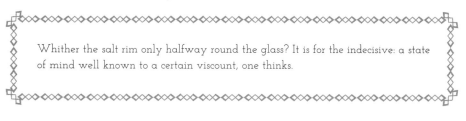

Whither the salt rim only halfway round the glass? It is for the indecisive: a state of mind well known to a certain viscount, one thinks.

# Wedding Breakfast

Here's a lovely and delightfully straightforward drink with which to toast the very mundaneness of a marriage that boasts no spectral patriarchs. Reader, before accepting a suitor's ring, one should thoroughly exhaust the subject of their intended's father—particularly if the relationship seems . . . complicated.

1 ounce (30 ml)
Salers aperitif liqueur

1 ounce (30 ml)
dry vermouth

1 ounce (30 ml)
lime juice

¾ ounce (22.5 ml)
simple syrup
(see page 21)

Ice-cold seltzer

Fill a highball glass nearly to the top with rocks cracked from a solid ice block, or 1-inch (2.5-cm) ice cubes, or a frozen spear of ice (see page 22). Combine the aperitif, vermouth, lime juice, and syrup in the base of a cocktail shaker. Add a medium-sized ice shard, lightly smashed into bits, or one or two cubes of ice; close the shaker and whip until the ice is nearly all melted. Add about 2 ounces (60 ml) seltzer to the shaker, then empty its contents, including any lingering ice, into the glass. If the cocktail doesn't rise nearly to the glass rim, add no more than about an ounce (30 ml) additional seltzer. Garnish with a pert bloom (or a lime wedge) and well-founded relief.

# Of Merriment & Mixed Drinks

One will have been schooled to believe one attends house parties purely for their matrimonial prospects, as at a house party, the itinerant attention of suitors is conveniently constrained to the company at hand. Such an innocent proposition belies the truth, however, which is that one attends house parties for the chance to participate in parlour games—in fact, in delightfully wicked parlour games, which is what ordinary parlour games become when one adds cocktails, a pact of secrecy, and the close proximity of dark hallways, unlit libraries, and even one's sleeping chambers.

Be not daunted! One has a good head and every right to enjoy oneself to the fullest degree—discreetly. But before packing one's valise and heading to the country, one should acquaint oneself with the basic rules for a few of the most popular entertainments.

## · SILHOUETTES ·

Darken the room but for the light of a single candle, which the silhouette sitter holds level with their shoulder, so that their shadow falls upon the wall behind them and their partner may trace it upon a piece of paper. How bold will one's pose become? Played in turns, in pairs, in separate rooms if need be. Pairs may be swapped.

## · WHO AM I? ·

Each player writes the name of one from the *ton* on a piece of paper. In turns, one draws a name, then must perform an impersonation—mannerisms and action only, no speech. One has but 30 seconds to play the part, and if one fails in their depiction, one must quaff their cocktail.

## · THE SCRIBBLER ·

Each member of the party is given a quill and writes five words on slips of paper, which are then put into a gentleman's hat. The hat is passed around, each person takes five slips, and then one has but five minutes to work their words into a rhyming verse—extra points for bawdy verbiage. When time is called, the verses are read aloud by a single player as the rest try to guess the scribbler. Guess correctly, and the scribbler must sip their cocktail. Guess incorrectly, however, and it is you who sips. Should the entire group be confounded, everyone but the scribbler drinks—again!

## · SECRET TOUCH ·

A chair is placed in the center of the room. In turns, one player is blindfolded, another placed in the chair, and the blindfolded player is led to them. They must then use naught but their hands to explore the body of the person in the chair—to see if they can guess their identity. The blindfolded person may speak, but the person in the chair must remain utterly silent, no matter what transpires.

## · PEAS IN A POD ·

All the lights are extinguished and one person is elected to go and hide. The rest of the party counts to an agreed-upon number, then splits up to try to find the hidden guest. When one finds them, one slips with them into their hiding spot, trying to be silent and still to avoid detection from any other players. Play continues until all but the last remaining seeker have wedged into the hider's secret spot. The last seeker becomes the next person to hide. As it is not uncommon for this game to dissipate into liaisons of opportunity, it is best played at the end of the evening.

*Have fun.*

## Chapter 5

# FOR MEMBERS ONLY

## SPIRITED DRINKS FROM THE CLUB

From Park Lane to Regent Street, in all of London there is hardly a door that is closed to me, and there are even fewer through which I have not dared to venture, both in and outside of Mayfield. But one sanctum ~~steadfastly~~ unreasonably denies me passage, reader. The gentleman's club.

This is vexing\*, because behind its impregnable doors, the club serves very good drinks. Planning grouse shoots and arranging marriages, gambling at dice, cavorting with opera singers—to whit, all the weighty affairs of the gentleman's world—require of him a stiffened spine. Thusly, at his club the gentleman lounges upon a leather throne, cosseted from unsolicited\*\* female trespass, sipping muscular cocktails of rather high potency. When I set out to learn the art of drinks, it was these potions I first pursued, determined to claim dominion over their secrets\*\*\*.

Now, they are mine to share\*\*\*\*.

---

\*Reader, this is infuriating! As is the struggle to constantly make light of one's subordination. (Pause for mixing of stiff drink.)

\*\*See previous observation about opera singers. The blameless souls. What choices do these women have?

\*\*\*As I am not allowed to own property.

\*\*\*\*Hah!

Some stiff drinks***** are built in the glass, and are nearly as virile as spirits sipped neat from the bottle: One serves them with a large rock of slowly melting ice. Others pair strong spirits with fortified wine and are chilled whilst gently stirring, so as not to too greatly dilute their strength. Both types have been known to unlock even a gentleman's fiercely guarded emotional kingdom******. Each is equally well known to occasion fighting*******. In short, they stir the soul—as few other drinks can.

Enjoy a certain club's purloined roster of spirited cocktails in the company of trusted companions. Tell secrets, plot conspiracies, speak imprudently********! Consider oneself in a club of one's own making, with membership of one's own choice! What a spirited act of rebellion.

*I submit herewith the roster of cocktails from a certain gentleman's club late of Grosvenor Square, London. Notations and amendments mine.*

---

# PISTOLS AT DAWN
## FOR THE GENTLEMAN OF HONOUR

2 ounces (60 ml) peated Scotch

¾ ounce (22.5 ml) sweet vermouth

¼ ounce (7.5 ml) Benedictine liqueur

2 dashes Angostura bitters

Add a medium-sized rock or a few 1-inch (2.5-cm) ice cubes
to a goblet glass. In a glass or crystal mixing vessel, gently stir
the whisky, vermouth, liqueur, and bitters with several large
rocks of ice until well chilled, about 25 to 30 stirs. Strain over
ice into the glass and garnish with candied cherries.

*This drink, a top performer on the club's roster, I herewith claim in honour of the unsung heroics of every woman who's ever thrown herself—metaphorically or otherwise—between two foolhardy gentlemen frankly and foolishly hell-bent upon their personal destruction. Honour, my foot.*

# Alleged Business

~~GOOD SIR~~

## ~~FOR THE FASTIDIOUS MASTER~~

1½ ounces (45 ml) gold Barbados rum

1½ ounces (45 ml) blanc vermouth

¼ ounce (7.5 ml) curaçao

In a glass or crystal mixing vessel, gently stir
the rum, vermouth, and curaçao with several large rocks of ice until
well chilled, about 25 to 30 stirs. Strain into a coupe glass and garnish
with an orange twist.

*And this one—a very cool and collected
quaff—I have renamed in tribute to
the ton's most ingenious and intrepid
mamas, whom no man should ever dare
to cross, lest he find himself suddenly. . .
called out of town.*

# VELVET COATTAILS

1½ ounces (45 ml) bourbon

¾ ounce (22.5 ml) Ramazzotti digestivo liqueur

¾ ounce (22.5 ml) Antica Carpano sweet vermouth

In a glass or crystal mixing vessel, gently stir the bourbon, digestivo, and vermouth with several large rocks of ice until well chilled, about 25 to 30 stirs. Strain into a coupe glass and garnish with an orange twist.

*Here is a drink named, I believe, in homage to the club's somewhat foppish clientele. It is a decent name, and so I let it stand, though foppish gentlemen are the <u>worst</u>. It is also a very nice drink, smooth and bittersweet.*

# DECENT SHOT
## A LETHAL COMBINATION

1 pint (16 ounces/480 ml) coppery-hued British pale ale

1 shot (about 1.5 ounces/44 ml) single- or blended-malt
Scotch, not peated

Serve the pint of ale cold alongside the shot of Scotch.
One either swallows the shot and then drinks the ale or pours
the shot into the ale and then consumes the two together.
The first is less gauche than the second.

*This is not truly a cocktail\*. And in a duel, let us be frank: No gentleman would <u>ever</u> refuse to fire their weapon, thus willingly and knowingly sacrificing their life as some sort of noble revenge token. I shall maintain that opinion unto my dying day.*

*It is, however, a delicious way to appreciate this combination of fruity and toasty malt flavours.

# PARSON'S MOUSETRAP

## ~~ONE'S FINAL TASTE OF FREEDOM~~

1⅛ ounces (45 ml) Irish whiskey

¾ ounce (22.5 ml) sweet vermouth

½ ounce (15 ml) green Chartreuse liqueur

2 dashes orange bitters

In a glass or crystal mixing vessel, gently stir
the whiskey, vermouth, liqueur, and bitters with several large
rocks of ice until well chilled, about 25 to 30 stirs. Strain
into a coupe glass and garnish with an orange twist.

*What a hilarious name. Did you know, reader, that this is how gentlemen mock the institution of marriage? The same institution that locks wives in a gilded cage whilst allowing husbands unadulterated sovereignty? They should call it the Prisoner's Dilemma. Again, though, lovely drink with subtle grassy flavours.*

# OXFORD SCHOOL CHUM

~~FOR HE OF KEEN MIND AND FELLOWSHIP~~

1 ounce (30 ml) rye whiskey

1 ounce (30 ml) dry vermouth

½ ounce (15 ml) Salers aperitif liqueur

½ ounce (15 ml) Benedictine liqueur

Place a single large rock or several 1-inch (2.5-cm) cubes in a
rocks glass. In a glass or crystal mixing vessel, gently stir the
whiskey, vermouth and liqueurs with several large rocks of ice
until well chilled, about 25 to 30 stirs. Strain over ice into
the glass and garnish with a lemon twist.

*Bloody hell. Does one even ~~realize~~
care how offensive this is to every female
in Britain, given that we're not allowed
to even dream of attending university?!
A crisp and faintly spicy drink.*

# CONTINENTAL TOUR

### ~~A SPIRITED SOUVENIR~~

1 barspoon absinthe

1½ ounces (45 ml) Cognac

¾ ounce (22.5 ml) sweet vermouth

¾ ounce (22.5 ml) Benedictine liqueur

1 dash Peychaud's bitters

Drizzle the absinthe into a coupe and swirl so the liqueur
coats the inside of the glass, then pour out the excess.
In a glass or crystal mixing vessel, gently stir the Cognac,
vermouth, liqueur, and bitters with several large rocks of ice
until well chilled, about 25 to 30 stirs. Strain into the coupe
and garnish with an orange twist and a candied cherry.

*Oh, to be a scion of society, perhaps a third or so son, upon whom much is lavished whilst little is expected. Travel! Study! Adventure! Go on and get thee to Greece, young master, but upon your return, should you find a dear (and maybe even beloved?) childhood friend at the doorstep of ruin—a grotesquely common occurrence when families boast more daughters than dowries—make haste to prove yourself, at minimum, a kind and supportive companion. And offer this drink, which is very refined and delicious.*

# BLOODSPORT

## ~~GETS ONE IN FIGHTING FORM~~

Pinch salt

1½ ounces (45 ml) Irish whiskey

½ ounce (15 ml) peated Scotch

½ ounce (15 ml) Ramazzotti digestivo liqueur

1 barspoon Drambuie liqueur

Place the pinch of salt into the bottom of a rocks glass and top with a
single large rock or several 1-inch (2.5-cm) cubes. Measure and pour
over the whiskey, Scotch, digestivo, and liqueur, then with a teaspoon,
gently stir the drink 5 or 6 times. Garnish with a lemon twist.

*To be clear, men's patriarchy over women
hinges on the fair sex being overly emotional,
erratic, and prone to poor decision making.
And yet, it is men who disrobe, step into
a padded ring, and willfully attempt to
pummel one another to death whilst other
men wager away their family fortunes on the
outcome, is it not? God help us all.*

# SECOND SON

1 barspoon absinthe

2 ounces (60 ml) rye whiskey

1 ounce (30 ml) sweet vermouth

¼ ounce (7.5 ml) Heering cherry liqueur

1 dash Angostura bitters

Drizzle the absinthe into a coupe and swirl so the liqueur coats the inside of the glass, then pour out the excess. In a glass or crystal mixing vessel, gently stir the whiskey, vermouth, cherry liqueur, and bitters with several large rocks of ice until well chilled, about 25 to 30 stirs. Strain into the coupe and garnish with a lemon twist.

*Just noting the rather high incidence of these spare heirs at the decadent soirées of my many artist friends. Coincidence? We typically talk art and peruse their drawings over this dewy drink.*

# REPREHENSIBLE ROGUE

## ~~FOR ONE'S DARKEST IMPULSES~~

1 ounce (30 ml) rye whiskey

1 ounce (30 ml) Cognac

¼ ounce (7.5 ml) Maraschino liqueur

1 dash Heering cherry liqueur (about ⅛ teaspoon)

1 dash absinthe (about ⅛ teaspoon)

2 dashes Peychaud's bitters

Place a single large rock or a few 1-inch (2.5-cm) cubes in a goblet.
Measure and pour over the whiskey, Cognac, liqueurs, absinthe,
and bitters, then with a teaspoon, gently stir the drink 5 or 6 times.
Garnish with a lemon twist.

*Now this drink, well, this one is one of my favorites.
And as it is also said to be favored by a certain viscount
of my unfortunate acquaintance, I should like to say
herewith—and before all memory of this unbecoming
episode passes\*—that when one cannot settle one's weak
and fickle mind regarding the fate of one's long-
suffering mistress, one should immediately take up this
glass and in its deep and abundant character, discover
what is <u>evidently</u> lacking in one's own.*

* By which I mean both the gentleman's all-too-typical tale and the three or so strong drinks I have
now imbibed . . .

# BACHELOR LODGINGS

### ─ENJOY IN IMMODERATION─

2¼ ounces (67.5 ml) Irish whiskey

½ ounce (15 ml) Benedictine liqueur

3 dashes Angostura bitters

Place a single large rock or several 1-inch (2.5-cm) cubes in a rocks glass.
Measure and pour over the whiskey, liqueur, and bitters, then with a teaspoon,
gently stir the drink 5 or 6 times. Garnish with an orange twist.

*Fine. I will not lie. I became quite good friends with a certain viscount's maliciously maltreated mistress (we met at a soirée outside Mayfield). She says that his pillow smells of cheese and that when he has had too many rounds of this stiff drink, his vaunted prowess has been known to abandon him.*

# LORD PROTECTOR

## ~~SATISFIES ONE'S EVERY DESIRE~~

Hearty bouquet of mint, no woody stems

2½ ounces (75 ml) Plymouth gin

¼ ounce (7.5 ml) simple syrup (see page 21)

Gently crush 8 to 10 sprigs of mint—just the tips—in your hands
to release their oils and aromas. Add them to a pewter mug or highball
glass, brushing the leaves down its sides to coat with the mint oils.
Pour the gin and simple syrup over the mint leaves and lightly muddle
to further bruise. Top with crushed ice (see page 88) until the cup
or mug is brimming, mounding as much ice on top as will stay put.
Stab a bouquet of mint sprigs—perhaps five or six, bundled together—
through the ice. Serve with a ~~metal straw.~~

*spike through the heart, more like.*

*Heartless and cold, just like this drink.
She. Deserved. Better.*

Object of My ~~Wrath~~ ~~Disdain~~ ~~Disapproval~~ ~~Affection?~~ Fatigue

# ~~LONG SHADOW~~

## ~~TO TOAST OUR GOOD SIRES~~

1½ ounces (45 ml) genever

1½ ounces (45 ml) sweet vermouth

1 barspoon Maraschino liqueur

2 dashes orange bitters

In a glass or crystal mixing vessel, gently stir the genever, vermouth, liqueur, and bitters with several large rocks of ice until well chilled, about 25 to 30 stirs. Strain into a coupe glass and garnish with a lemon twist.

Dear Certain Viscount,

Given your callous, imperious, and quite frankly reprehensible attitude toward the women in your life, it is my earnest belief that you may well be beyond salvation, your charming sideburns and dashing manner notwithstanding. You do not deserve this delightful drink—though it is a bit nutty, which one could also most kindly say of yourself.

from here forward, drinks my own

# Menace to Society*

Dearest Inevitable Object of a Certain Viscount's Untrustworthy Intentions (Given His Probable Inability to Evade Marriage Entirely or Indefinitely),

Whoever you may be, should you become enamoured with this rogue, I fear you are destined for a tumultuous love affair. Should you therefore require the shoulder of a true friend to cry upon, or entry to a drawing room that is exceedingly well equipped to nurse one's embattled and ransacked emotions, please do not hesitate to call upon me. In anticipation, I have created for you, <u>myself</u>, this bitter and complicated cocktail, and dedicate it in your honour, with best wishes for your unscathed extrication from any ill-advised entanglements.

1 ounce (30 ml) Plymouth gin

1½ ounces (45 ml) Salers aperitif liqueur

1 ounce (30 ml) blanc vermouth

2 dashes lemon bitters

1 dash orange bitters

Place a single large rock or several 1-inch (2.5-cm) cubes in a rocks glass. Measure and pour over the gin, aperitif, vermouth, and bitters, then with a teaspoon, gently stir the drink 5 or 6 times. Garnish with a grapefruit twist.

*The gentleman is all this and more. Though one can only imagine he'd say the same of you, should you prove a woman of your own mind, resistant to his "charms." The viscount is particularly affected by sensible females.

# Den of Iniquity

This one is for you, Terrifying Dowager—my dearest, kindest, most cherished friend. <u>Thank you</u> for encouraging me to write this book. I am quite certain I have now mired the entire endeavour in utter ruin. I did so try to rein myself in, and yet here one is, overcome like a debutante after her first Champagne. It is all, sometimes, just too much. I know you know. I shall see you at the next meeting of our own private club, and we shall enjoy this impish sip together. Provided I have not been required to leave the city on alleged business.

—LJ

**2 ounces (60 ml) peaty Scotch**

**¼ ounce (7.5 ml) falernum liqueur**

**2 dashes Angostura bitters**

Place a single large rock or several 1-inch (2.5-cm) cubes in a rocks glass. Measure and pour the Scotch, liqueur, and bitters over the ice, then with a teaspoon, gently stir the drink 5 or 6 times. Garnish with a lemon twist.

## Chapter 6

# PRIVATE ASSIGNATIONS

### TIPPLES FOR TWO

A very wise but rather intimidating friend of mine is nevertheless known to say that "love conquers all." Reader, I am as fascinated by the ton's happily-ever-after stories as anyone, but to that I say, bollocks. Allow me to recount my own history of love. Right up until its end, it is a rather common tale.

I hoped for a love match, as does every innocent debutante. I behaved decorously, devoted myself to my training, and held my tongue. In my first season, I was courted and had suitors, but no proposals. In my second season, a gentleman offered me his hand (after a rather lukewarm romance), but then married his distant cousin, whose father unexpectedly ascended to a title and fortune. Throughout my third season, I stayed in my room, where I proceeded to make acquaintance with my own . . . mind. My fourth season, with help from my dear, true, and terrifying friend, I was married.

Reader, as marriages go, it is not actually a terrible marriage. My husband leaves me be (he has other interests), and I am comfortable enough. I have not yet been blessed with children, but one never knows. I seek my liberty wherever I can.

My cherished friend, helping me to organize my thoughts for this book, suggested I include a chapter of drinks for couples. "The ones that taste like romance in a glass of cut crystal," she said, a wicked gleam in her eye.

"The sweet ones, then?" I asked. "You have one and find you are full and finished?" Reader, she whacked me with her damnable walking stick.

However, as I do truly owe her everything, yes, fine. Let us have a chapter of sweet cocktails for couples. But I insist we stretch the parameters of "couples" and "romance" to be more accommodating. The *ton* has enough ridiculous rules to last one <u>several</u> lifetimes. So by all means, enjoy a sweet or sweetish cocktail with one's true love—or with one's paramour, or a mysterious and discreet stranger, or an illicit lover, or one's companion of convenience. Limit not oneself, reader. And by the same token, enjoy any of these delectable drinks with one's dearest friend, or one's recent acquaintance, or one's brother or sister or mama or papa, or even one's very own self, alone. All love affairs have value, as does every being on this Earth. This is hardly a popular opinion here in the second decade of the nineteenth century. But if my dearest friend is right, and love—however one defines it—truly <u>does</u> conquer all, well then I suppose we shall see.

# Secret Missive

When one and one's lover must be physically separated, one should take inspiration from a notorious gossip columnist and explore the unexpected pleasure of putting quill to paper. Mix up this intoxicating quaff, settle betwixt one's sheets, and record all of one's most intimate longings. Neither letter nor cocktail is a treat easily forgotten.

1½ ounces (45 ml) Pusser's rum

¾ ounce (22.5 ml) falernum liqueur

¾ ounce (22.5 ml) lime juice

½ ounce (15 ml) honey syrup (see page 43)

1 dash Angosturo bitters

Combine the rum, liqueur, lime juice, syrup, and bitters in the base of a cocktail shaker. Add a generous quantity of large ice cubes, close the shaker, and shake vigorously for 15 to 20 seconds. Fine strain into a coupe glass. Garnish with a lime twist.

# Secret Ruse

Perhaps one has experienced curious stirrings whilst having one's chemise strings pulled by one's lady's maid? Reader, be assured: It is as natural to enjoy the female touch as it is to crave this soft and supple tipple. Alas, given the narrow mores of our society, one shall have to look beyond the polite circles of the *ton* (or one's household staff) for satisfaction. Write me, as I am happy to serve as one's emissary in this pursuit.

1½ ounces (45 ml) rye

¼ ounce (7.5 ml)
Cinnamon Syrup
(see page 157)

1 ounce (30 ml)
Fresh Pineapple Syrup
(see page 159)

½ ounce (15 ml)
heavy cream

1 egg

2 dashes Angostura
bitters

Combine the rye, syrups, cream, egg, and bitters in the base of a cocktail shaker. Cap the shaker and shake for about 15 seconds, until the mixture is frothy—this is called "dry shaking." Uncap and add a generous quantity of large ice cubes, close the shaker, and shake vigorously for at least 15 to 20 seconds more. Fine strain into a coupe glass. Dust a fine sprinkling of nutmeg across the surface, and add, perhaps, a delicate floating violet.

When one "dry shakes" a cocktail without ice, one begins to lighten and froth the mixture of egg and cream, trapping air that ultimately gives these rich and luscious cocktails their velvety texture. Should one skip the dry shake and proceed immediately with ice, to create the same foamy effect one would have to shake the drink much, much longer, and by that time, the drink will have become a lank and overly diluted disaster. And that is a terrible tragedy.

# Dark Walk

I may also be of some assistance to any gentleman who has found himself lingering about a moonlit garden, longing for a glimpse of a certain dashing duke. Content oneself with this sultry sip whilst we work through the pertinent introductions.

**1½ ounces (45 ml) Ramazzotti digestivo liqueur**

**¾ ounce (22.5 ml) Cognac**

**½ ounce (15 ml) lemon juice**

**¼ ounce (7.5 ml) simple syrup (see page 21)**

Combine the digestivo, Cognac, lemon juice, and syrup in the base of a cocktail shaker. Add a generous quantity of large ice cubes, close the shaker, and shake vigorously for 15 to 20 seconds. Fine strain into a coupe glass.

My first taste of Ramazzotti—a dark and bitter Italian liqueur—was whilst sitting on a nobleman's terrace in Milan. We sipped it with ice after dining, as is the custom (thus why it is considered a "digestivo"), and from the first, I knew its orange and earthy notes would be haunting in cocktails. If one cannot find it, err on the dark side with another Italian digestivo, preferably one with similar citrusy character.

# Gretna Green

A pillow of cream floats across the top of this dreamy little cocktail like a bride's wedding dress puddled upon the carriage floor. Which is precisely how one should pass the excruciatingly long carriage ride to Scotland: in a state of reckless, repeated, utter, thorough, and completely <u>exhausting</u> scandal.

2 ounces (60 ml)
peated Scotch

¾ ounce (22.5 ml)
honey syrup
(see page 43)

1 ounce (30 ml)
heavy cream

¼ ounce (7.5 ml)
simple syrup
(see page 21)

In a glass or crystal mixing vessel, gently stir the Scotch and honey syrup with several large rocks of ice until well chilled, about 25 to 30 stirs. Strain into a coupe glass. Combine the cream and simple syrup in the base of a cocktail shaker. Add one not-too-big ice cube, close the shaker, and shake vigorously for about 15 seconds, until the cream is airy and light and the ice has melted. Pour or spoon the frothy cream gently over the top of the cocktail and let it drift across the surface.

For a cream float, one wants the cream merely aerated and lightened, not churned nearly to butter. If one is intimidated by the shaker, instead add about 2 to 3 ounces (60 to 90 ml) cold cream and about ½ ounce (15 ml) simple syrup to a small jar, cap it, and shake vigorously until the cream is frothy, also about 15 seconds. When one is just learning this technique, the small jar may be easier to manipulate.

# Improper Conversation

If, in addition to her embroidery and household management, a debutante should learn to breathlessly whisper salacious suggestions into a suitor's ear, she will become a very happy and fulfilled wife indeed. This frothy and frolicsome quaff has proven a favourite amongst couples exploring the pleasures of advanced wordplay.

1¾ ounces (22.5 ml) Old Tom gin

¼ ounce (7.5 ml) absinthe

½ ounce (15 ml) simple syrup (see page 21)

½ ounce (15 ml) heavy cream

White of 1 egg (about ¾–1 ounce/22.5–30 ml)

Combine the gin, absinthe, syrup, cream, and egg white in the base of a cocktail shaker. Cap the shaker and dry shake vigorously for about 15 seconds, until the mixture is frothy. Uncap and add a generous quantity of large ice cubes, close the shaker, and shake vigorously for at least 15 to 20 seconds more. Fine strain into a coupe glass or goblet. Although one commonly garnishes drinks made with cream and egg with a sprinkling of spice, here one wants the absinthe flavour to shine. Try florals like geranium or pansy petals instead, to splash against the drink's creamy white backdrop.

# Sparring Partner

One grudgingly admits that the rather infectious strain of spirited banter passing between a certain viscount and the new and unexpectedly unconventional object* of his heretofore-entirely-unreliable affections often signifies nearly unbearable chemistry, possibly even respect. In fact, it puts one in mind of this lively and refreshing cocktail, of which one frankly never tires.

¾ ounce (22.5 ml) Plymouth gin

¾ ounce (22.5 ml) green Chartreuse liqueur

¾ ounce (22.5 ml) Maraschino liqueur

¾ ounce (22.5 ml) lime juice

Combine the gin, liqueurs, and lime juice in the base of a cocktail shaker. Add a generous quantity of large ice cubes, close the shaker, and shake vigorously for 15 to 20 seconds. Fine strain into a coupe glass. Garnish with a candied cherry.

*Did I not predict a "romance" (of some sort) was inevitable? One's astuteness is one's curse.

# Silken Coverlet

Embellished tea towels or a set of silver cutlery is traditionally considered a proper wedding gift. I give the recipe for this alluring cocktail. It is as naughty as a lace-trimmed negligee and nearly as conducive to bringing little heirs and debutantes into the world.

1½ ounces (45 ml) Old Tom gin

¾ ounce (22.5 ml) lemon juice

¾ ounce (22.5 ml) Fresh Raspberry Syrup (page 157)

White of 1 egg (about ¾–1 ounce/22.5–30 ml)

Combine the gin, lemon juice, raspberry syrup, and egg white in the base of a cocktail shaker. Cap the shaker and dry shake for about 15 seconds, until the mixture is frothy. Uncap and add a generous quantity of large ice cubes, close the shaker, and shake vigorously for at least 15 to 20 seconds more. Fine strain into a coupe glass.

The cap on a drink made with egg whites is almost like the meringue on a tart. To succeed, it is essential that one dry shake with great vigour—if the mixture doesn't look airy and bubbly, shake longer and harder before adding ice. And once ice is added, the second shake should be firm and delivered with total commitment.

# Thunderclap

Whilst a certain viscount entertains a party at his country seat, I've been as keen as anyone to hear all the sensational* tattle. But, reader, I confess: The spate of surprisingly tender tales issuing forth has, instead, rather undone** (some of) my most deeply held convictions on the subject of ~~romance~~ the certain viscount. And as such, I find myself taking to my bed with this cocktail, and the unfamiliar pangs of what one assumes is, possibly, (dare I say it?) a mix of envy and admiration. Which, reader, is proving to be a somewhat potent combination.

2 ounces (60 ml)
rye whiskey

¾ ounce (22.5 ml)
simple syrup
(see page 21)

¾ ounce (22.5 ml)
lemon juice

White of 1 egg (about
¾–1 ounce/22.5–30 ml)

½ ounce (15 ml)
ruby red port

Place a single large rock or several 1-inch (2.5 cm) cubes in a rocks glass. Combine the whiskey, syrup, lemon juice, and egg white in the base of a cocktail shaker. Cap the shaker and dry shake for about 15 seconds, until the mixture is frothy. Uncap and add a generous quantity of large ice cubes, close the shaker, and shake vigorously for at least 15 seconds. Fine strain over ice into the rocks glass. Grasp a barspoon in one hand and hold it with its back-side up, just above the surface of the cocktail. Slowly, so as not to splash it into the drink, pour the port over the back of the spoon so it breaks through the drink's froth but then floats in a layer between foam cap and cocktail. Sit back in a state of (annoyed? remorseful?) bemusement and . . . ponder.

*As in surprise-filled, and not in a good way.

**Well, let's be fair and say loosened.

# Love Match

Here's a drink that feels just like . . . well, I believe it has been called one's "pinnacle." It's a luscious and sweet quaff topped with the airiest, lightest poof. Which just keeps growing as one pours a stream of delightfully fizzy sparkle into the mix.

**2 ounces (60 ml) Cognac**

**¾ ounce (22.5 ml) lemon juice**

**¾ ounce (22.5 ml) simple syrup (see page 21)**

**White of 1 egg (about ¾–1 ounce/22.5–30 ml)**

**Ice-cold Champagne**

Combine the Cognac, lemon juice, syrup, and egg white in the base of a cocktail shaker. Cap the shaker and dry shake for about 15 seconds, until the mixture is frothy. Uncap and add a generous quantity of large ice cubes, close the shaker, and shake vigorously for at least 15 to 20 seconds. Fine strain into a flute. Add about 2 ounces (60 ml) Champagne, until the froth nearly crests over the rim.

To push the poof up the glass, the Champagne must stream gently down the side of the glass. Hold the flute at an angle whilst pouring, and barely touch the Champagne bottle to the inside rim of the glass.

# ‘Burning Questions

Dearest Blushing Debutantes,

If one found oneself in a state of warm and flustered confusion whilst reading any of the previous notations, brew up two of these edifying concoctions and tell one's mama one would appreciate her company immediately for a <u>very</u> important, very frank conversation.

**3 ounces (90 ml) strongly brewed black tea**

**2 ounces (60 ml) genever**

**½ ounce (15 ml) Cinnamon Syrup (see page 157)**

**1 barspoon Fresh Ginger Syrup (see page 158)**

**¾ ounce (22.5 ml) lemon juice**

Bring an ample quantity of water to a boil. Pour some into a teacup to warm it, as if one was preparing a cup of tea. Use a further 8 ounces (240 ml) to steep a strong brew of black tea—preferably in a small warmed kettle, to keep the tea piping hot. Then, create a warming receptacle for the base of one's shaker: A bowl of boiling hot water will do. Measure the genever, syrups, and lemon juice into the base and stir until the solution is well warmed. Empty the hot water from the warmed teacup, add 3 ounces (90 ml) piping hot black tea, then pour in the warmed spirits. Garnish with a thinly sliced lemon wheel and one's determination not to accept any euphemistic explanations.

# Compromising Position

An astonishing new development in the story of the viscount and the surprising object of his fickle affections! If the latest rumour is true and an indisputable scandal has transpired in broad daylight . . . well then the darling girl deserves a nip of this lusty little quaff. Though whether in victory, sympathy, or sabotage, one remains entirely unsure—if one is being honest.

1 ounce (30 ml)
gold Barbados rum

1 ounce (30 ml)
Pusser's rum

1 ounce (30 ml)
Honey Syrup
(see page 43)

¾ ounce (22.5 ml)
heavy cream

Combine the rums, syrup, and cream in the base of a cocktail shaker. Add a generous quantity of large ice cubes, close the shaker, and shake vigorously for 15 to 20 seconds, until very frothy. Fine strain into a coupe glass. Garnish with a very light sprinkling of grated cinnamon.

# Rake's ~~Revenge~~ ~~Rescue~~ ~~Revenge~~ ~~Rescue~~ Revenge

Reader, when I am wrong—or may be wrong, or not, or may, or . . . (what is happening to me?!)—I say so. And as the tale of his romantic odyssey continues to unfold, I am willing to entertain the possibility that, with regards to the viscount, I <u>may</u> have judged too harshly. It could be that, in the arms of the right woman (damn her), a roguish scoundrel has another side entirely. One that is as frothy and milky-sweet as this demure-but-with-a-dark-side cocktail. Whilst also remaining pleasingly spicy. And possessed of such tremendous sideburns. And flirtatious eyes. And tempting lips. And strapping, muscular thighs . . .

1½ ounces (45 ml) genever

¾ ounce (22.5 ml) Maraschino liqueur

¾ ounce (22.5 ml) simple syrup (see page 21)

¾ ounce (22.5 ml) heavy cream

1 cardamom pod, crushed with the flat of a knife

Place a single large rock or several 1-inch (2.5-cm) cubes in a rocks glass. Combine the genever, liqueur, syrup, cream, and the crushed cardamom pod in the base of a cocktail shaker. Add a generous quantity of large ice cubes, close the shaker, and shake vigorously for 15 to 20 seconds, until very frothy. Fine strain into the rocks glass. Serve with a sigh emanating from the very depths of one's soul.

## Epilogue

# POLITE COMPANY

### COCKTAILS SANS SPIRITS

Dear Lady Thornwood,

I have been enjoying your book! It was sent to me by a certain terrifying dowager of our mutual fondness and admiration. When I am not . . . busy ~~with~~ with the duke, I hope to develop some adroitness with cocktails myself. But I also believe that I may be with child with some fequency throughout the near and foreseeable future! Browsing through these recipes, one chafes at the thought of drinking naught but weak tea and lemonade for nine months at a stretch. What do you recommend?

With affection,
    The Duchess

My Dearest Duchess,

I am so grateful for your note. You do know there are things a woman can do to prevent a man's seed from taking root, do you not? What am I saying—of course you don't. I am happy to explain, speaking as a scientist. We shall discuss.

Meanwhile, as a cocktail maker, I can assure you that you need not be deprived of delightful drinks during your indubitably frequent confinements. Here are several recipes for fizzy drinks that are every bit as quaffable as their spirited counterparts. They're made with delicious flavoured syrups, and as the syrups are useful in potent cocktails, too, when one has finished procreating, be sure to try them in that capacity.

—LT

# The Right Honourable

For the thrill-seeking husband who, nevertheless, is prudent about gambling away the family fortune.

◆ ◆ ◆

**1½ ounces (45 ml) Honey-Tea Syrup (page 158)**

**¾ ounce (22.5 ml) Fresh Ginger Syrup (page 158)**

**1 ounce (30 ml) lemon juice**

**6-8 (180-240) ounces tonic water**

**Lemon wedge, for garnish**

# Pampered Lap Dog

Inspired by one of Queen Charlotte's bitches. The one who is also a notorious gossip, I believe.

◆ ◆ ◆

**2½ ounces (75 ml) Fresh Raspberry Syrup (page 153)**

**1½ ounces (45 ml) lime juice**

**6-8 ounces (180-240 ml) seltzer**

**Sprig of mint, for garnish**

# Gently Bred Lady

Looks pale and demure but conceals a ruthlessly
bitter streak. Very refreshing.

✦✦✦

**3 ounces (90 ml) grapefruit juice**

**½ ounce (15 ml) lemon juice**

**½ ounce (15 ml) simple syrup (see page 21)**

**6-8 ounces (180-240 ml) tonic water**

**Curl of grapefruit peel, for garnish**

# Unimpeachable Virtue

Made from the rarest of fruits, to celebrate the rarest of qualities.

✦✦✦

**3-4 ounces (90-120 ml) Fresh Pineapple Syrup (page 159)**

**1 ounce (30 ml) Cinnamon Syrup (page 157)**

**½ ounce (15 ml) lemon juice**

**Pinch salt**

**6-8 ounces (180-240 ml) seltzer**

**Freshly plucked pineapple frond, for garnish**

To make a fizzy drink, one simply combines flavoured syrup and juice in a high-ball glass filled with crushed ice (see page 88) or 1-inch (2.5-cm) ice cubes. The syrup is topped with either seltzer or tonic water, one stirs, and then with a final garnish, the drink is accomplished. Refreshment proceeds apace.

# THE SYRUP LARDER

As drink mixing evolves, the most intrepid mixers have realized that simple sugar syrups are themselves opportunities for creativity, and a way to add more flavour and nuance to drinks. I keep a jar of simple syrup (made of equal parts sugar and boiling water) on hand at all times. But when the garden bursts with fresh fruits and herbs, or I hear of an exotic new ingredient coming off the ships and into the shops, my first thought is to preserve its flavour in a syrup.

There are two basic methods for making syrups. The first is to infuse a simple syrup with more flavour, as if one was making tea. Each of the recipes below is an infusion. The other is to mix simple syrup with other ingredients, commonly pureed fruit, to make a compound syrup, then strain it to remove any pulp. The primary difference between the two is that compound syrups, even after straining, are heavier-bodied and rich, containing both fruit sugars and the syrup's sugar.

Which leads us to the science of syrups and drink making. Generally, one uses syrups in drinks made with the shaking technique, as the trapped air and bubbles balance the syrup's density. One's tongue is also less adept at discerning sweet flavours in ice-cold mixtures. Subsequently, the coldest, most aerated drinks both require and will tolerate the most sweetness. When one is experimenting with cocktails—perhaps modifying the recipes of this very book—if one keeps these principles in mind, one will soon find themselves adept. As one drinks maker to another, that is my highest aim.

# Fresh Raspberry Syrup

**MAKES ABOUT 20 OUNCES (600 ML)**

**2 cups (250 g) fresh raspberries, rinsed**

**8 ounces (240 ml) water**

**1 cup (200 g) sugar**

Put the raspberries and water in a small pot and bring them to a boil on the stove. Quiet the flame so the mixture is just barely simmering and let it cook gently about 5 minutes. Strain the mixture through a sieve placed over a bowl. Then strain a second time with cheesecloth or another thin filter in the sieve, pressing on the raspberries to extract as much juice as possible. Discard the mashed raspberries. Whilst the mixture is hot, add the sugar and stir to dissolve. Pour the syrup into a jar and store, chilled, for up to one week.

When making syrups containing fruit or other perishable ingredients, if a small amount of alcohol is not a concern, one may add a spoonful or two of gin to extend the syrup's life for 2 to 3 weeks longer.

# Cinnamon Syrup

**MAKES ABOUT 16 OUNCES (480 ML)**

**2–3 cinnamon sticks**

**8 ounces (240 ml) water**

**1 cup (100 g) sugar**

Put the cinnamon sticks and water in a small pot and bring them to a boil on the stovetop. Add the sugar and stir until it is dissolved. Take the mixture off the flame, pour into a container, cover and set aside for 12 hours. Strain the syrup into a jar through a cheesecloth or another thin filter set in a sieve. Store, chilled, for up to one month.

# Fresh Ginger Syrup

**MAKES ABOUT 12 OUNCES (360 ML)**

6 ounces (170 g) fresh ginger, washed but unpeeled

6 ounces (170 g) sugar

6 ounces (180 ml) water

Cut the ginger root into pieces about the length of one's thumb. With the flat of a knife, smash the lengths of ginger, then chop very finely. Combine with the sugar and set aside overnight: The mixture will turn syrupy. When ready to proceed, put the sugar and ginger mixture in a small pot with the water and bring it to a boil. Remove from the flame and strain through a cheesecloth or another thin filter set into a sieve over a bowl, pressing on the ginger to extract as much syrup and juice as possible. Pour the syrup into a jar and store, chilled, for up to one week.

# Honey-Tea Syrup

**MAKES ABOUT 8 OUNCES (240 ML)**

4 ounces (120 ml) strongly brewed black tea, hot

8 ounces (240 ml) honey

Combine the hot tea and honey in a jar and shake or stir until combined.

One needn't limit themselves to black tea. One is, after all, English. Experiment with jasmine, oolong, darjeeling, or the bergamot-infused black tea one hears the Earl of Howick Hall, Mr. Grey, serves. One could also make this syrup without honey by combining the brewed tea with an equal amount of sugar.

# Fresh Pineapple Syrup

**MAKES ABOUT 12 OUNCES (360 ML)**

**1 pineapple, trimmed and peeled**

**12 ounces (360 ml) simple syrup (made with 2 cups/ 400 g sugar and 2 cups/480 ml water; see page 21)**

Cut the pineapple in half through its length, then cut each half through its length to create quarters. Cut out the core of each wedge, then slice the wedges into triangles. Put these into a large bowl with the simple syrup and keep cold for at least 6 hours and up to one full day, pressing with the back of a spoon from time to time to mash the juices from the fruit. Pour the pineapple and syrup through a cheesecloth or another thin filter set into a sieve over a bowl, pressing on the pineapple to extract as much syrup and juice as possible. Pour the syrup into a jar and store, chilled, for up to one week.

Letting one's exotic pineapple rot upon the table in a state of admiration is abominably wasteful. Juice it for punch or preserve its sweetness in a syrup, then slip its long fronds—which one plucks from the crown—into fizzy highball-style drinks as garnishes.

Dear Lady Thornwood,

Whilst reading your delightful book, I came across your pointed reference to uninspired lemonade tables and found myself fretful, as I suspect in the past mine has been woefully lacking. But from ignorance, not privation or parsimony! I would like my lemonade table to be the talk of the ton—in a good way. Especially as I am hosting a soirée in the near future and hope to make a good impression upon a certain gossip columnist. I have both a young suitor and a debutante on the marriage mart this season, and each could use a bit of a bump. I shall be serving your sparkling cocktails and one of this book's delightful punches. How should one equip one's lemonade table?

Yours with gratitude,
An Aspiring Cunning Mama

Dear Aspiring Cunning Mama,

I am very flattered, and advise you to cease with fretting. We shall remedy the testy subject of your lemonade table in short order. Here is what I recommend.

First, one needn't limit oneself to pallid lemonade. See my above note to the duchess regarding fizzy drinks prepared without spirits. Were any of these types of drinks to be served at your ball, my carriage and I would happily stay put.

If one is still determined to serve lemonade, I have suggestions to that end, as well. And as the most egregious errors made at the lemonade table actually have to do with service and ice, we shall address those problems forthwith.

Wishing you a successful ball, a most favourable mention in a certain gossip column, and advantageous matches for your progeny,


Lady Thornwood

# REFINED REFRESHMENT

One never wants a long queue at one's lemonade table—a slew of agitated mamas in a single spot for an indeterminate length of time spells disaster. Subsequently, one wants the drinks to be poured and served quite quickly.

For fizzy drinks, this means batching all of the base ingredients together so that at service, all that must be done is for a server to pour a set quantity of chilled mix into a highball glass and top with ice-cold seltzer or tonic (plus a garnish: Have it pre-cut, or else use something like a flower or herb sprig).

## To Batch

Multiply each ingredient by the number of drinks you wish to make, mix all these together in a large receptacle, then divide into some lovely glass bottles and chill.

## To Serve

Pour out the number of ounces in the base recipe.

For example, Unimpeachable Virtue has a base of 4½ ounces (135 ml), so one would pour 4½ ounces (135 ml) of syrup over ice in a highball glass, then top with seltzer and a pineapple frond. Very quick and simple.

If one does not have servers at the table, one should put out the chilled bottles of syrup alongside bottles of ice-cold tonic and seltzer and a Champagne bucket or punchbowl filled with ice, and create a charming instruction card explaining how one assembles one's own drink. To whit, for the Unimpeachable Virtue:

*Fill one's glass one-third full of syrup.*
*Add ice. Top with seltzer.*

The problem with ice, of course, is that it melts and dilutes one's drink. Therefore, one should always keep ice and drinks separate, adding ice only when the drink is poured.

For service, I recommend using solid 1-inch (2.5-cm) cubes of ice, or the largest size of solid ice that will fit into your drink glass, as these will melt more slowly in the ice bucket or punchbowl. For highball glasses, one can even use a specially shaped mold and freeze ice in rectangular spears nearly the length of one's glass. Regardless of the size of one's service ice in the punch bowl, one should also nest a large solid block of ice beneath it to keep the set-up as chilled as possible. Refresh frequently throughout the service.

If one forgoes fizzy drinks for lemonade, one should treat the lemonade like punch and serve it in a punchbowl, well-chilled with a decorative round or block of ice (refer to my instructions on page 57). Here is my recipe for a basic lemonade:

# Lemonade

## SERVES ABOUT 32

◆ ◆ ◆

**1 recipe simple syrup, made with 4 cups (400 g) sugar and 4 cups (960 ml) water (see page 21)**

**4 cups (960 ml) lemon juice (from about 20 lemons)**

**2 gallons (32 cups/7.5 liters) water or seltzer**

To make this more memorable, replace the simple syrup with an equal quantity of infused or compound syrup: Try the raspberry syrup on page 157, or a strawberry compound syrup perhaps, or a tart cherry compound syrup. Amongst flavoured lemonades, my particular favourites are those made with herb-infused syrups, like this one shown opposite, which one can also use in combination with a fruit syrup (about three-quarters fruit to one-quarter herb syrup) to extraordinary effect.

One lemon, squeezed, will provide one with about 1½ ounces (45 ml) fresh juice. For both lemonade and cocktails, freshly squeezed juice is first-rate, but note that freshly squeezed juice will keep, chilled, for about 8 hours before it begins to turn and lose its brightness. A drink made with juice that is more than 12 hours old is a tragedy.

# Tarragon-Mint Syrup

### MAKES ABOUT 8 OUNCES (240 ML)

8 ounces (240 ml) water

1 cup (100 g) sugar

5 sprigs fresh tarragon, rinsed

3 sprigs fresh mint, rinsed

Put the water and herbs in a small pot and bring it to a boil. Turn off the heat and add the sugar, stirring to dissolve. Let steep 15 minutes. Strain through a cheesecloth or another filter set into a sieve over a jar, pressing on the herbs. Keep in cool storage.

Dear Lady Thornwood,

I must be developing a taste for outspoken women. I have read your book, and I am not sure if I find you captivating or insufferable. That being said, I decided to divert myself with an amusement wherein I downed a dram of Scotch each time I found myself appearing in your text. As some of your allusions were quite transparent, I grew rather drunk. And the next morning, Mama's lady's maid foisted upon me a concoction of eggs and garlic most vile, by way of remedy for my lingering ills and bad humour. There must be a better tonic. I am assuming you have a recommendation, as you seem to have an opinion about everything.

The "Certain" Viscount

Dear Certain Viscount,

Not one word in recompense on the subject of our long-flown songbird? You remain, sir, a callow cad.

Nonetheless, yes, I can do better. And am ~~happy pleased~~ compelled to provide you with the following recipe, since as a drinks maker, I believe it is my duty to spread their art. Feel free to share it with your companions.

As for yourself, one continues to hope you become worthy of your immense good fortune,


Lady Thornwood

**16 ounces (480 ml) tomato juice**

**2 ounces (60 ml) hot sauce**

**1 ounce (30 ml) Worcestershire sauce**

**1–2 teaspoons prepared horseradish**

**1–2 ounces (30–60 ml) tamari**

**1–2 ounces (30–60 ml) green olive or capers brine**

Mix in a small pitcher, adjusting ingredients to taste. Serve over 1-inch (2.5-cm) ice cubes in highball glasses, garnished with a lemon wedge and several green olives impaled on a skewer. If one's malady is grave to the point that spirits are required, add 2 ounces (60 ml) gin to each glass.

P.S. If, on the other hand, you should find yourself returning to your former shameful habits, send me a missive. We can discuss our mutual loathing over a cocktail.

—LJ

# NOTES AND ACKNOWLEDGMENTS

Lady Thornwood's book of drinks—set approximately in 1815, post battle of Waterloo, and midway through the Regency era of 1795 to 1837—accepts a (very) few anachronisms within her ingredients. The Luxardo distillery was not founded until 1891, but the family had been making and perfecting the recipe for Maraschino liqueur for almost a decade. Peter Heering's small shop, where he sold his proprietary "Cherry Cordial," was founded in Copenhagen in 1818, just a few years after Lady Thornwood's writing—but he first began to ply his trade in 1815. Salers Aperitif La Bounoux Gentiane Liqueur is the oldest branded gentiane liqueur, first bottled at the Distillerie de la Salers In 1885. But the good lady correctly states that gentian liqueurs were common throughout France, Switzerland, and Germany for almost a century prior. Allspice dram and falernum, similarly, became part of cocktail consciousness in the 1930s and 1940s, embraced by drinks makers exploring the flavors of the Caribbean after the end of Prohibition. But in Lady Thornwood's time, both were traditional elixirs that had been known, made, and imbibed in Jamaica and Barbados, respectively, for centuries.

Lady Thornwood, being an open-minded woman keenly interested in all aspects of scientific discovery and the natural universe, has also dabbled in the occult and the realms of clairvoyance. Thusly, her book draws upon a handful of recipes that would be published years later by other writers. To whit: Duty & Desire (page 43) is an Airmail, first documented in *Handbook for Hosts* in 1949; Diamond of the Season (page 45) is an amended French 75, a drink first credited to Harry MacElhone of Harry's New York Bar in Paris in 1915; Diamond in the Rough (page 46) is a London Buck, first published in *The Savoy Cocktail Book* by Harry Craddock in 1930; Scribbling Woman (page 52) is a Death in the Afternoon, a cocktail by the writer Ernest Hemingway; the drinks Family Jewels (page 42), Satin Knee Breeches (page 49), and Worthy Suitor (page 50) are what are known as "royale" versions (topped with Champagne) of the Bijoux (*Harry Johnson's New & Improved Bartender's Manual*, 1882), Tuxedo (*Harry Johnson's New & Improved Bartender's Manual*, 1882), and Rusty Nail (Club 21, New York City, 1950s) cocktails, respectively; Terrifying Dowager (page 66) is an adaptation of a classic Daniel Webster punch; Incorrigible Gossip (page 69) is an adaptation of a classic Regent's Punch; Country Seat (page 88) is a classic Cobbler, which originated in the 1830s; Distant Cousin (page 90) is an Adonis (Waldorf-Astoria Hotel, New York City, 1884) made with Manzanilla sherry; Pistols at Dawn (page 111) is a Bobby Burns from *The Savoy Cocktail Book* by Harry Craddock in 1930, but made with peated Scotch; Alleged Business (page 112) is an El Presidente from the 1924 *Manual del Cantinero*; Second Son (page 119) is a Remember the Maine from Charles H. Baker Jr.'s *Gentlemen's Companion*, 1939, but with an absinthe rinse; Lord Protector (page 122) is a gin Mint Julep, which is commonly called a Major Bailey, here made with Plymouth gin; Object of My Fatigue (page 123) is a classic Martinez, here made with genever; Gretna Green (page 136) is an Athol Brose, a legendary Scottish quaff first adapted and published in Charles H. Baker Jr.'s *Gentlemen's Companion* in 1939, here made with peated Scotch; Sparring Partner (page 139) is a Last Word, first published in *Bottom's Up!* by Ted Saucier in 1951; Silken Coverlet (page 140) is an adaptation of a Clover Club from the Bellevue-Stratford Hotel in Philadelphia in the 1880s; Thunderclap (page 143) is an adaptation of a New York Sour from the 1880s; and Love Match (page 144) is a classic Fizz made with Cognac. One must give credit where credit is due, and in the world of cocktails, one is always drawing inspiration from the work of others, tweaking and finessing ingredients to make a drink one's own.

Many thanks are herein owed to Anthony Schmidt, who taught me the art of drinks, and Arsalun Tafazoli, who was crazy enough to give me two full years of employment to write a five-hundred-plus-page training manual for Consortium Holdings on the making of cocktails and the history of booze. Thanks also to Rica Allannic of the David Black Literary Agency, who ignited the spark that became this work, Laura Dozier and Shannon Kelly and the team at Abrams who thought it could be done and made it a reality, and illustrator extraordinaire Niege Borges, who gave it vivid, wild life.

Of course, one must also thank a certain streaming service and content platform—and its amazing team of writers, directors, actors, costumers, etc., ad infinitum—for bringing the adapted Grosvenor Square universe of author Julia Quinn to our small screens in the form of *Bridgerton* during one of the most jarring, discombobulating periods of recent world history, inspiring the creation of this book. What would one have done without Regency-era scandal, bodice-ripping, and eye candy to keep one's spirits up during such a fraught time? This book was written with all due haste whilst in the middle of selling one's house and getting ready to move cross-country for graduate school, and one is ever thankful for the encouraging, patient, and kind support of one's beloved family. Greg, Indiana, and Scarlett Schaefer, who inspire one to be as much like Lady Thornwood as one dares. Ever onward.

ABOUT THE ^other^ AUTHOR

Amy Finley's great-grandfather was a turn-of-the-century saloon keeper. Until the pandemic, she was the in-house drinks writer for San Diego hospitality group Consortium Holdings, whose drinks den and boutique bottle shop, Raised by Wolves, made *Esquire* magazine's 2019 Best Bars in America list, and whose apothecary-styled cocktail bar, Polite Provisions, was *Imbibe* magazine's Bar of the Year and a James Beard Award nominee. She is also the author of the memoir *How to Eat a Small Country* (2011). Her writing has appeared in *Bon Appétit*, *Departures*, and *Good Housekeeping*. She currently lives in Vermont.

Editor: Shannon Kelly
Designer: Diane Shaw
Managing Editor: Mike Richards
Production Manager: Sarah Masterson Hally

Library of Congress Control Number: 2021934853

ISBN: 978-1-4197-5924-6
eISBN: 978-1-64700-559-7

Printed and bound in the United States
10 9 8 7 6 5 4 3 2 1

Abrams Image books are available at special discounts when purchased in quantity for premiums and promotions as well as fundraising or educational use. Special editions can also be created to specification. For details, contact specialsales@abramsbooks.com or the address below.

Abrams Image® is a registered trademark of Harry N. Abrams, Inc.

**ABRAMS** The Art of Books
195 Broadway, New York, NY 10007
abramsbooks.com